RACIST STATES OF MIND

RACIST STATES OF MIND
Understanding the Perversion of Curiosity and Concern

Narendra Keval

Routledge
Taylor & Francis Group

LONDON AND NEW YORK

First published 2016 by Karnac Books Ltd.

Published 2018 by Routledge
2 Park Square, Milton Park, Abingdon, Oxon OX14 4RN
711 Third Avenue, New York, NY 10017, USA

Routledge is an imprint of the Taylor & Francis Group, an informa business

British Library Cataloguing in Publication Data

A C.I.P. for this book is available from the British Library

ISBN-13: 9781780490748 (pbk)

Typeset by Medlar Publishing Solutions Pvt Ltd, India

For
Tanuja and Niah

CONTENTS

ABOUT THE AUTHOR

Narendra Keval is an adult and adolescent psychotherapist with a background in clinical psychology. He worked as a specialist in psychoanalytic psychotherapy in the NHS and other outpatient settings, working in particular with patients suffering from complex personality disorders. He has done consultancy and training work both in the NHS and organisations in the private sector. He was clinical director on the doctoral program in clinical psychology at the University of East Anglia and senior lecturer at the Centre for Psychoanalytic Studies, University of Essex. He is currently a visiting lecturer at the Tavistock Clinic and in full-time private practice.

But such is the irresistible nature of truth that all it asks,
and all it wants, is the liberty of appearing.
(Thomas Paine, 1737–1809)

ACKNOWLEDGEMENTS

All thinking is relational in nature involving conversation. There have been many conversations about racism that have been percolating in my mind over the years, both personal and professional, with people from all walks of life. These have ultimately shaped the way I have thought and written about racism in this book. My interest in this subject goes back to memories of growing up in Zambia, Africa, formerly the British colony of Northern Rhodesia. The words "coloured quarters" and "curfews" were mentioned casually in conversation, yet the true power of these words were elusive, woven into the normal fabric of everyday life. Their imprint was unconsciously known, but not fully thought about or articulated. Perhaps this experience of the unthought known motivated me to investigate racism in depth many years later.

This work has been made possible by my patients, who have allowed me access into the privacy of their minds to gain a deeper understanding of the human vulnerabilities that drive racist thinking and feeling. While I am grateful for the privilege of working with them, they have to remain anonymous.

I would like to acknowledge my parents whose tenacity and resilience through their own migrant journeys and struggles, continues to be a source of inspiration and support in my work. Supervisors and mentors in both the adolescent and adult departments of the Tavistock Clinic, too many to mention individually, have in their different ways equipped me with the tools to analyse racism. I want to thank them all. I must acknowledge Shireen Visram for the emotional support she offered me when I started out as a psychotherapist and which continues to sustain my personal and professional life. I am most grateful to her. I also want to thank the late Jafar Kareem and colleagues at the Nafsiyat Intercultural Therapy Centre, for their generous collaboration in thinking about the impact of the racist imagination on the psyche of patients from the Black and other minority ethnic communities.

I am grateful to my colleagues in Cape Town, South Africa for inviting me to their professional forums, during my sabbatical, where we shared many difficult and thought-provoking conversations about race which have stayed with me. In particular, I want to thank the Cape Town Society for Psychoanalytic Psychotherapy, the Trauma Centre, University of Cape Town, University of Western Cape, and the Direct Action Centre for Peace and Memory. Having the opportunity to teach and supervise students both here in the UK and in South Africa has been another vital source of ideas. I thank them all.

I am especially grateful to John Keene for his comments on earlier drafts of the manuscript and for his generosity of spirit in the professional support and mentoring he has provided over the years. I want to thank Ivan Ward for both his critical engagement with the ideas in the book and editorial help that shaped the manuscript. The staff team at Karnac Books, particularly Rod Tweedy, Tom Hawking, Constance Govindin, and Cecily Blench are to be thanked for their patience, encouragement, and support throughout this project.

This book would not have been possible without the emotional support and patience of my wife Tanuja and our daughter Niah, who have been on this journey with me since the inception of this book. It is to them that I give my deepest thanks.

Not unlike some of the challenges in the subject matter of this book, its identity has evolved through new encounters with peoples, places, and ideas that created opportunities and discoveries which helped me develop the ideas contained herein. In the spirit of the book, I hope that the reader's own sense of curiosity will stir up a wish to debate some of my ideas about this disturbing and tragic human phenomenon.

London, December 2015

A NOTE REGARDING PRONOUNS

There are occasions in the text where the personal pronouns used in hypothetical situations lean towards the masculine (i.e., "he", "him", and "his"). Where the flow of the text permits, the pronouns of both genders are used in tandem (e.g., "his or hers"). Therefore, the overuse of male pronouns is not indicative of any discrimination towards the masculine, but rather a prosaic device to avoid wordiness.

INTRODUCTION

Identity is a complex tapestry. Offering a sense of integrity and continuity on one level, it is also hybrid in nature, creating disruption and multiplicity. As we move fluidly in our psychic identifications and geographically from one place to another so we are inextricably linked and connected. Such connections and hybridity offend the sensibilities of the racist imagination, which strives only to create myths of purity that only exist in our wishful thinking for absolute certainties. The problem for racism is that all human encounters are potentially transformative, which no ethnic categorisation could possibly capture.

A central theme explored in this book is that these myths are entrenched beliefs that strongly resist any mixture with the new and different, their principal aim being to obliterate linking, meaning, and even life itself. Inextricably linked with the vicissitudes of social life, their predatory and opportunistic nature also make these beliefs extremely resistant to change.

Racism is a treacherous phenomenon with many faces, and it shows a remarkable capacity to co-exist with support for ethnic and cultural diversity. Its character is subtle, sly, and cunning, and like a chameleon can transform itself in ways that make it difficult if not impossible to prove its existence. In its visible forms it can be a mean-spirited absence of reciprocity or mutuality—or something more violent, seeking only to appropriate, to colonise the fruits of others' labour, attacking potency in mind and body. To be at the receiving end of this type of animosity is to experience something that cuts deep and gnaws away subtly at your sense of self, sometimes signalled by a visceral response that something is not quite right, a feeling in the guts that one has been, or is being, misused. Racism can curtail the fullest freedom of the mind of the individual, group, and society.

This book is an attempt to explore and understand some of the unconscious mechanisms and processes that underpin this phenomenon by looking at racism as a state of mind, inferred from the clinical situation and racist situations in the external world. From this perspective, racism is a particular mental state amongst many others that can be brought into play to cope with the demands of everyday life, which raises interesting questions about the use of this mental state and not another. Under what conditions might it be used, and what purpose is it meant to serve emotionally and socio-politically? What internal and external conditions influence the movement in and out of these states? The whole phenomenon raises interesting challenges for the therapist about how one might speak to these states of mind in ways that facilitate a movement towards more humane ways of relating to the self and others.

My observations have been anchored in the experience of working clinically with these states of mind in the consulting room and using these observations to understand wider processes in group, organisational, and societal life. This is not meant to imply that the trajectory of explanation is unidirectional, from inner to outer world, because the clinical situation is always socially embedded and not something "pure" that is "applied" to explain the external world. As a clinician, it was simply my starting point of investigation. Perhaps the way this book has been organised into three parts speaks to the character of the phenomenon, which weaves in and out between the social and individual, each giving shape to the other.

The psychoanalytic method enables unconscious narratives to be identified through fantasies whose meanings can be closely tracked, explored, and understood behind the manifest content of words. Gestures, behaviours, images, symbols, and dreams also have an emotional impact on the therapist and are used by him in the therapeutic encounter. Whether this method sufficiently accounts for different forms of racism—from the brutality of racism on the street to more sophisticated versions which we may encounter in the consulting room or in institutional life—is an interesting question. I would argue that focusing on the unconscious narratives of racism provides a bridge across these different forms to capture the complex nuances of the lived reality.

In psychoanalysis, the dominant modes of explanation for racism is couched in the form of splitting and projective processes, within a paranoid-schizoid mindset. It is, however, worth bearing in mind that these are not explanations of racism as such, but psychic and inter-personal processes that are operating within complex narratives.[1] For example, projecting denigrated aspects of the self into another person or group gives emotional distance from the responsibility of thinking about these qualities in oneself. It gives relief to the perpetrator but pain to the victim, who is burdened with the split-off parts of the perpe-trator, denying him his true identity. These processes are operating to enact hatred and revenge within a wider narrative of an imaginary love and betrayal in racism. They are explored in the opening chapter where racism's preoccupations concretely equate the geography of the psyche and nationhood. Segments of Enoch Powell's "rivers of blood" speech are dissected to understand the fantasies behind a central feeling in rac-ism, that of being psychically robbed or depleted. These accusations are laid firmly at the door of the ethnic other, but the unconscious narrative suggests that the grievance is also directed at an imaginary couple in the shadows.

Vengeful wishes emanating from this grievance involve a regressive fantasy of return to a mythical structure that is often gendered into the notion of a pure and idealised maternal space, free of perceived intru-sions from a world of difference and diversity. This defence against the third dimension precludes an Oedipal triangular configuration, or a space that allows for spontaneity in thinking and feeling, but involves painful feelings of loss unravelling a sense of the familiar.

Chapter Two elaborates on these themes to arrive at a working for-mulation by looking at the notion of the "racist scene", symbolic of the wider-body politic of racism, in order to understand key themes and drivers in racist states of mind. It situates them within a conceptual framework of the primal scene, which is used as an overarching frame-work for positioning some of the most salient themes, struggles, and predicaments encountered in racist states of mind. The intermingling of both benign and malignant elements in the primal scene fantasy is used to understand the emotional turmoil in racism, where both scenes share common elements that need to be understood more closely. These involve both pre-Oedipal and Oedipal anxieties that come to bear on what Freud (1908c) described as the nuclear complex. I use this framework to explore how curiosity and concern are perverted to maintain grievances that thwart the "ethnic other" in racism and sidestep painful feelings of loss and mourning that an acknowledgement of diversity and differences bring forth.

The dictum appears to be "you have robbed me and for that you shall pay in the way that I will rob you". Thus the racist intent aims to deny any pleasures of life and living to the ethnic other. But what is the nature of this loss that converts raw grief effortlessly into hatred? As introduced in the opening chapter, the overt grievance in racism is that a geographical place, time, customs, traditions, or a sense of the familiar has been robbed and lost forever. The racist state of mind does not accept this fact of life. Instead, it strives in an endless pursuit to recover what is lost through an ideology that aims to expunge ethnic others and seek an imagined utopia at the cost of thwarting their desires and emotional freedom.

Chapter Three takes the reader into the second part of the book, focusing on issues of race as they emerge in the clinical situation. My intention here is to understand racial superiority as one of the many defences used in the functioning of a pathological organisation in the personality (Steiner, 1993) that can obstruct recognition of human vulnerability, need, dependency, and desire itself.

The case material hopes to illustrate some of the main themes and struggles encountered in engaging with these troubling, and troubled, states of mind. Patient stories are complex, and in highlighting certain dynamics and themes others have been given less prominence, but they are no less relevant or important to the cases described. Neither were the snapshots of case material of an individual or series of sessions intended to be representative of the whole treatment period with the patient.

None of the patients described here came for help because they were worried about their propensity for racism; in fact, this is unlikely to be the case in any clinical practice. Rather, it was a discovery made through the analytic work of understanding unconscious obstacles in the patient's mind. Racist states of mind were one of these obstacles, in contrast to, perhaps paradoxically and surprisingly, "racial fantasies", by which I mean preoccupations about the ethnicity of others which are driven more by an unconscious desire to know or get to know that may be used in the service of growth and development of the self.

I doubt if anybody would set foot in my consulting room if these beliefs have become a permanent fixture in their personality. Nevertheless, the racist imagination that my patients have struggled with reflects the general malaise of our society in the way it uses minor differences to retreat into a sense of superiority over others. How the patient's inner world hooks into this strategy of defence to serve particular functions in the ego at different moments of the treatment was of prime interest and concern.

Most analysts and therapists will have encountered these mental states in their patients irrespective of whether they manifest themselves within an ethnic or racial dimension, where what is essentially human is relentlessly dehumanised by mechanisms involving omnipotence, covert thuggery, and violence. This type of brutality from the patient raises difficult therapeutic challenges for the therapist, whose task is to remain robust and empathic in the hope that the patient can gradually feel strong enough to resist turning to a racist solution for their difficulties. This is difficult to do when the very need for the therapist to be of independent mind, so as to assist the patient to engage with their vulnerabilities, enrages them like a red rag to a bull.

Some of the difficulties of engaging clinically with these mental states are further considered in Chapter Four, looking at the experience of being at the receiving end of the racist gaze, which various clinicians have commented on since the seminal work by Fanon (1952). I focus on three areas of interest to me. First, the traumatising aspects of both overt and covert racist assaults on the psyche that thwarts the capacity for freedom of movement in the mind. Second, I show that this type of psychic paralysis can present itself in ways that invite the therapist to bear witness. Often the visceral nature of the assault is too difficult to think about and articulate, but the effects of its imprint on the mind and body continues to seek expression. To witness and name the experience is to act as a potent participant-observer who catalyses the patient into reclaiming a vitality in the self that was deadened by this type of assault. It requires a capacity in the therapist to be both observer and observed in a triangular space that can enable the victim to establish distance from the racist gaze that has become internalised.

I consider further complexities that can arise when racist assaults link up with particular facets of the individual's character to bring fresh life to earlier terrors connected with traumatic ruptures in the continuity of self. These become re-enacted, creating challenges for the therapist, namely the struggles to retain a capacity to continue thinking, feeling, and remaining curious about the patient in the face of pressures to re-enact the very dynamics that underpin these toxic states of mind.

Chapter Five looks at some of the theoretical and clinical problems that arise in engaging with issues to do with race and racism, looking at the difficulties of mitigating potential re-enactments of some of the very dynamics of racism in conceptualising this work. Fantasies of ethnic matching, particular facets of therapist ethnicity and counter-transference pressures are brought alive clinically. This is in the context of a Black patient whose struggles with being a victim and perpetrator of racism took on a particular poignancy when the menacing nature of the racist object in his inner world surfaced with a vengeance in the wish to attack both his and my skin colour.

Chapter Six takes us into the third part of the book, which looks at unconscious racism beyond the consulting room into group, organisational, and societal life, where these states of mind can emerge quite suddenly and forcefully. Locating this problem within a framework of understanding societal and organisational defences against anxiety make psychoanalytic institutions no exception in their vulnerability to becoming caught up in these subtle dynamics. I suggest that the evidence for this comes from the lack of adequate representation of people from Black and other ethnic communities within the profession, which mirrors structural racism in society.

One possibility I consider is of a natural "fault line" within the body of psychoanalysis that may create vulnerabilities to repetition of the trauma of having been an object of historical denigration at the hands of the anti-Semitic, Viennese, non-Jewish establishments. The persecution that eventually unfolded in the "ethnic cleansing" and genocide of the Jews in Europe led many analysts to become displaced refugees. I suggest that this dynamic may be expressed in a displaced form by marginalising and cleansing the ethnic other out from its own domain of inquiry and practice, creating a type of unconscious apartheid.

How some of these processes can play out institutionally, even if only tentatively understood, is illustrated through vignettes that speak to the subjective experience of being in organisations where thinking about ethnicity and racism in training or professional practice is particularly difficult to do. It leaves the subject matter, experience, and the participants uncontained and even cleansed-out.

Chapter Seven describes my experience of consulting to a study group that regressed into creating an adolescent mental life as a defence against working through the pains and pleasures of acquiring a secure professional identity. I look at how the racialisation of anxiety about the new and different in the "group mind" started to take on a potentially paranoid, menacing, and violent direction into targeting and ganging up on my "thinking-black head". It echoes the effortless way in which racial and cultural differences can be seized upon and targeted with precision. When more constructive forces were able to hold sway in the direction of experiencing elements of guilt, curiosity and concern, this enabled the group to steer themselves back on task, and for real learning to proceed.

Chapter Eight looks at the emotional impact of a decision to introduce an ethnically diverse food menu and sanction a separate group for Black patients in an organisation that cared for severely mentally-ill people. The organisational naivety behind these decisions, which effectively involved the "immigration" of new ideas or different foods into the existing canteen menu for fragile patients was met with the type of paranoid anxieties and racist solutions that mirror contemporary struggles to engage with issues such as immigration and ethnic diversity in our society. As societies become part of a global village, with continual movement of peoples across geographical borders and territories, this creates challenges in how hidden and not-so-hidden grievances are grappled with, when raw grief from real or imagined losses turn to hatred in the fertile ground of the racist imagination.

Chapter Nine looks at the struggles between the forces of reason and racism, a dichotomy which is itself problematic given that "rationality" has been historically located in the Enlightenment project from where much of "race thinking" arose, powering the colonial mentality of "civilising" others. I am thinking here about a collusive and corrupt relationship between reason and racism that is both gratifying and has opportunistic motives which remain hidden in the dichotomy. The case material described here suggests that while there are threats of thuggery and violence if loyalty to the racist organisation is betrayed, the patient also took sadistic pleasure from it.

It is not too surprising to learn that when these defences are breached and exposed there is much to contend with. Here my focus was on how society manages what it may feel as a betrayal or ambush of reason when the racist impulse breaks out unexpectedly in an individual or organisation. The frantic or manic atmosphere, which often prevails in the immediate aftermath to restore what has been ambushed by this public and private exposure, works against potentially reparative processes borne out of a sense of guilt and concern.

Where gross racist violence is involved, as in the particular case of the murder of the Black teenager Stephen Lawrence in 1999, I suggest that it is highly probable that the destructiveness of the racist and sadistic violence (as portrayed by the perpetrator's rants) infected and became systemically enacted using the fertile ground offered by the less extreme "culture of racism" of the Metropolitan Police Force. These essentially attacked all reasonable attempts to keep the investigation on track and bring the perpetrators to justice. A further tragedy ensued in the way systemic failures frustrated and thwarted the Lawrence family, exposing them to further pain, repeating the type of traumatic assault that takes place in racism.

In the concluding section, I sketch out key ideas that emerged in my mind while writing this book, and their implications for thinking about contemporary struggles with racism in society. The astonishing intransigence of racism is a reminder of the observation that human beings have a strong propensity for suspicion and cruelty towards strangers and, as Freud (1930) repeated as an evident truth, with the weight of history on his side, "man is a wolf to man" (p. 111). While this warns us against promulgating fables about human nature that seek straightforward solutions to racism, my clinical examples suggest that it is the capacity to continue thinking in the face of unreason that is ultimately the ongoing container for grappling with racism. The reparative power of psychoanalysis is in the potential it offers to be a potent witness not only to the grievances that fuel the acrimony and cruelty of racism but also to hear those on the receiving end who have lost the courage to be outraged enough and be able to rediscover a vitality of spirit that was damaged by racism.

Some parallels inevitably came to mind, such as the nature of grievances and the quality of thinking in racism, fundamentalism, and terrorism. Perhaps all three mind-states highlight the therapeutic and societal challenges of how to continue thinking in a way that accommodates the other when the very existence of the other is the grievance. Murder is then felt to be the only solution, chillingly portrayed by one of my patients whose terms of relating to me insisted on an abortion of any fruitful outcome that could arise from "mixing our minds".

Throughout this book, various terms such as race, ethnic, racial, Black, or Asian have been used, which will evoke certain sensitivities and controversies surrounding their suitability, for which there is no straightforward solution except a willingness to debate their use. I decided to use the term "ethnic other" throughout the book because it feels more flexible and inclusive of all cultures and denotes the fact that we are all ethnically located, irrespective of our skin colour and backgrounds (Hall, 1992). The unconscious motivation for the racialisation of ethnic others is what this book hopes to explore. All case material has been appropriately disguised to protect the patients' privacy without compromising the issues I am trying to explore and understand.

PART I

THE PSYCHIC GEOGRAPHY OF RACISM

CHAPTER ONE

Mythical homelands: body, psyche, and nation

> ... the misfortunes of the subject did not start the day the breast
> was withdrawn from his lips (Masotta, 1976); it is the very
> process of being lost forever that counts.
>
> (Kohon, 1986, p. 60)

We all have the potential to be racist. Racist hatred can be effortlessly discharged with either brute force or, more subtly, through complex unconscious processes and enactments. These manifest interpersonally as well as structurally or institutionally in our society to create catastrophic emotional, social, and economic consequences for those at the receiving end. Racism is not created solely out of external societal structures nor is it a purely psychic phenomenon, but rather both shape and call upon each other in the service of different functions. This suggests a complex, interactive relationship between individuals, their immediate social groups, and, more widely, to societal spaces and structures. In other words, the phenomenon serves particular functions in the psychic economy of the individual, group, and society.

Kovel's (1970) seminal work highlights the sheer tenacity and intransigence of racism that is collectively enacted by society in the way it organises its spaces and institutions, which are often racialised through splitting and projective processes. Steinbeck's (1939) classic novel "The Grapes of Wrath" is a poignant example of how dismal economic conditions and a poverty of circumstance can often lead to a poverty of thinking and feeling. Psyche and society can link up in a lethal mixture such that tribal or ethnic hatreds erupt in an effortless and opportunistic way in otherwise ordinary people. Once the "Okkies" (migrants from Oklahoma) are dispossessed of their home and belongings they are converted in the imagination of their Californian hosts from ordinary folk, looking for work and a sense of home, to dirty animals invading the Californian landscape. This tribal encounter is experienced internally and socially in the hosts as a contamination that has to be simply cleansed and evacuated, avoiding any acknowledgement of human feelings or moral struggles to be engaged, lived, and worked with.

Anybody who has participated in a group-relations event will recognise the shocking ease with which human beings can exploit socio-political lines of cleavage or boundary markers, such as ethnicity, class, or gender, to project powerful thoughts and feelings into others. Paranoid anxieties can be lodged with precision into an out-group (Bion, 1961). I was struck by the effortless nature of this process in the immediate aftermath of the terrorist attacks on September 11th 2001 and July 7th 2005, when thinking about others who are ethnically different had a tendency to get lodged in the private and public imagination with a sense of panic and terror. Quite unbearable anxieties became stirred up at a personal, national, and global level, with the deadly combination of both real and imagined threats to our lives. I recall my increased vigilance on the London underground in the immediate aftermath of the attacks, where I had unwittingly joined the mindset in which everybody was a potential suspect. In this atmosphere, the capacity to discriminate and think humanely of fellow citizens is hijacked by what I call a racist state of mind, which is quick to expel and lodge the anxiety outside the self rather than process it. The shooting of an innocent man by counter-terrorist police at Stockwell underground station may have been a further tragic outcome of this mindset and the tendency to panic that it engenders.

Patient A

A Black patient of mine spoke about his first taste of racism in the school playground when he left the West Indies for Britain as a young teenager. A couple of White boys proceeded to mock his skin colour which escalated into a frightening and menacing atmosphere when they formed a gang to get hold of his arm to etch their hatred by repeatedly scratching it, shouting and laughing while he was in pain. "Look," they said, "this black bastard is white underneath". It was an anxious but triumphant laugh as the violence escalated; the more the young Black man was in pain from the sudden and brutal assault on his self, the more they laughed.

In the intimacy of the consulting room the patient wished to communicate to me the distress of his trauma in the school playground, which now linked up in his mind with an emerging fear of my presence and of the potential intrusion of the analytic process. Was our inquiry going to be as brutal as his experience in the playground in uncovering and understanding the difficulties that brought him to see me? In this narrative was also a developmental story that needed to be understood in the context of his own conflicts between leaving his native home and coming to a different land, to a future of possibilities, only to be met, in the throes of his early adolescence, with hatred and violence.

The White teenagers' encounter with this young man's black skin colour was experienced as something internally intolerable which could not be contained and was expelled in a violent way by attacking the youngster. But what was it that was so internally intolerable that it found an immediate hook in the external world by targeting the black skin of this young man? Perhaps it communicated how ill-contained they felt in their own skin in the face of change that was signalled by the arrival of a visually different person. Where did he come from? How did he get there? Why is he here in my space? These were young men also in the throes of their early adolescence—a time of tumultuous change in mind and body, a time of omnipotence and vulnerability—conflicted with a wish to remain children yet move forward in their development. There is a strange embrace within this conflict, in the form of a hateful intimacy, when the arm of the young black man is grabbed to create a violent breach of his body boundary. Why should the enigmas of adolescent development take this particular route?

My patient appeared to have got caught up in a complex process of projective identification (Klein, 1946), where he became an opportunistic target for a conflict residing in the internal world of the White youngsters. When they saw the "whiteness" underneath his black skin, this in some way reassured them that there was nothing to worry about—he was the same as them. In other words, the victim of their attack reassures *them* that there is no rupture in the continuity of their own sense of self, and no painful feelings of loss that are too difficult to manage.

The physicality of the young man's black skin became a stage on which a developmental drama was being played out. It was an old narrative about psychic change and loss, being the same and different, revivified in the form of racial hostility. In this way, perhaps the attempt was to get my patient to experience what they were experiencing internally—an assault on their own sense of self in the form of a developmental turmoil that they could not bear to experience. What was intolerable within the self was racialised and expressed as white intolerance of the black, who became a convenient hook on which to hang their feelings (Hinshelwood, 2007).

What is concealed in this conversion of anxiety to violence is the bewildering kaleidoscope of feelings that encounters with the ethnic other can potentially stir up, particularly feelings of being narcissistically injured. Attempts at mastery of these wounds through the triumph of sadism left the Black teenager as the casualty of a perverse pleasure that had also gained momentum. Their response to the sense of bewilderment—"look, this black bastard is white underneath"—masked a small movement that could have potentially paved a way towards curiosity and their common humanity behind the sudden discovery that he was, after all, the same human being as them. This was, however, lost to the triumph of violence that ensued at the cost of a traumatic rupture in identity, which the young Black man was forced to experience through the attack on his skin and mind.

This suggests that the racist state of mind is one that has experienced psychic injuries that it forces the victim of racism to experience in a "tit-for-tat" manner. We need only look at some of the themes that surface in the politics of identity when the race or immigration card emerges approaching election time to know that bewilderment about psychic/social change and feelings of loss are at the heart of this wounding; so too is the need for restoration fantasies that convey a sense of fragility of geographical boundaries and borders that need protection from politicians in the face of an imagined flood of foreigners who are perceived to be depleting the community or nation.

These themes are echoed in the infamous and disturbing "rivers of blood" speech given by Enoch Powell to a Conservative association in Birmingham on April 20th 1968. It was a criticism of Commonwealth immigration and proposed anti-discrimination legislation which portrayed the immigrant as an unwelcome stranger causing psychic and social mayhem to an idealised English landscape and social order. What was ignored in the rhetoric of "purity" and "homogeneity" were class and regional conflicts within Britain itself and the fact that immigration policy had actively encouraged migrants from abroad to live and work in the UK to make up for the shortage of labour, particularly in the service sector. I have selected segments of this speech that point to themes that are of particular relevance here.

> In fifteen or twenty years, on present trends, there will be in this country three and a half million Commonwealth immigrants and their descendants ... *Whole areas, towns and parts of towns across England will be occupied by sections of the immigrant and immigrant-descended population* ...
>
> It almost passes belief that at this moment twenty or thirty additional immigrant children are arriving from overseas in Wolverhampton alone every week—and that means fifteen or twenty additional families a decade or two hence. *Those whom the gods wish to destroy, they first make mad ... It is like watching a nation busily engaged in heaping up its own funeral pyre.* So insane are we that we actually permit unmarried persons to immigrate for the purpose of founding a family with spouses and fiancés whom they have never seen ...
>
> *The discrimination and the deprivation, the sense of alarm and of resentment*, lies not with the immigrant population but with those among whom they have come and are still coming ...
>
> But while, to the immigrant, entry to this country was admission to privileges and opportunities eagerly sought, the impact upon the existing population was very different. ... *they found themselves made strangers in their own country* ... They found their wives unable to obtain hospital beds in childbirth, their children unable to obtain school places, their homes and neighbourhoods changed beyond recognition, their plans and prospects for the future defeated ... *as time went by, more and more voices which told them that they were now the unwanted.* They now learn that a one-way privilege is to be established by Act of Parliament; a law which cannot, and is not intended to, operate to protect them or redress their grievances is to be enacted to give the stranger, the disgruntled and the agent provocateur the power to pillory them for their private actions ...

Eight years ago in a respectable street in Wolverhampton a house was sold to a Negro. Now only one white (a woman old-age pensioner) lives there … *Then the immigrants moved in. With growing fear, she saw one house after another taken over. The quiet street became a place of noise and confusion.* Regretfully, her white tenants moved out …

We are on the verge here of a change … Now we are seeing the growth of positive forces acting against integration, of vested interests in the preservation and sharpening of racial and religious differences, *with a view to the exercise of actual domination, first over fellow-immigrants and then over the rest of the population.* The cloud no bigger than a man's hand, that can so rapidly overcast the sky, has been visible recently in Wolverhampton and has shown *signs of spreading quickly …*

For these *dangerous and divisive elements* the legislation proposed in the Race Relations Bill is the very pabulum they need to flourish. Here is the means of showing that the immigrant communities can organise to consolidate their members, to agitate and campaign against their fellow citizens, *and to overawe and dominate* the rest with the legal weapons which the ignorant and the ill-informed have provided. As I look ahead, *I am filled with foreboding; like the Roman, I seem to see "the River Tiber foaming with much blood".* (Powell, 1968, my italics)

Despite the storm of protest across Britain after the speech, an opinion poll by the Gallup research organisation showed that seventy-four per cent agreed with the sentiments expressed in Powell's speech. His rhetoric managed to touch fertile ground in the British psyche, triggering paranoid anxieties of being swamped or flooded, or being "ganged up" on by a large herd or group, anxieties that we are once again witnessing in the recent refugee crises (2015) that have created a systemic reaction which some have called "Fortress Europe". What struck me about Powell's speech was how its hysterical quality could easily provoke a wish to overlook the profound sense of loss that is being alluded to in a feeling of "what once was and is no longer"—a universal theme. He is, however, consumed by it, unable to stomach it as if it was eating him up from the inside, so much so that, looking at it today, he seemed to be foaming at the mouth like the river Tiber in his speech. He gives us clues to this internal revolt expressed in the sense of grievance of being marginalised, unwanted, and essentially deprived, while ethnic others are perceived to be enjoying privileges or pleasure, culminating in a feeling of being robbed.

Powell's solution to repatriate the foreigners tells us something about how easily raw grief is converted into hatred and a wish for revenge, as he goes about proposing an evacuation of the ethnic other from the psyche and society as a means of soothing the psychological hurts and injuries through a fantasy of restoration. This involves de-contaminating an imagined utopia, freeing it from the painful feelings of loss and grief that would have to be worked-through in accommodating the ethnic other. As his speech implies, to accommodate the other, and face up to the painful work of mourning, would be tantamount to a descent into madness and suicidal despair.

The speech conveys racism's preoccupation that concretely equates the physical body or presence of the ethnic other with psyche and nationhood—an equation that is clearly evident on the current international stage, where geographical spaces and boundaries arouse such primitive passions (Said, 2003). These often contain elements related to fantasies and feelings which belong to "quite another scene" (Cohen, 1993, p. 12)—an idealised place free of imaginary intrusions (Reicher & Hopkins, 2001) that is often gendered into notions of motherland or Mother Earth, our first geographical and psychical home (Freud, 1930).

Restoration fantasies promote a nostalgic gaze towards an imagined or re-imagined protective community that will soothe the hurts and injuries attributed to the arrival of the ethnic other. They attempt to restore the individual or community to a former state of completeness, but it is a delusional idea that it is possible to return to this mythical homeland as a solution to profound anxiety.

Gadd's (2010) sociological work speaks to some of these themes when he suggests that racist hatred is a function of a complex melding of hidden injuries and hurts arising from traumatic ruptures of relationships in an individual's past with those of class-based injustices (e.g., unemployment through industrial decline leading to loss of community/income/pride/potency, etc.), resulting in a profound sense of loss. Rejections and humiliations in one domain of experience both reinforce and are reinforced by those in another. These multi-layered losses can culminate in grievances and hatreds that coalesce and find expression in a predatory, socially sanctioned, and opportunistic structure in racism, which serves to bind all the emotional turmoil that is locked into melancholic responses.

This formulation and others that situate racist hatred within the turmoil of socio-cultural melancholia (Gilroy, 2006a) point to, but do not sufficiently explore, layers of losses which require closer scrutiny.

Freud speaks to these other scenes in his classic work "Mourning and Melancholia" (1917):

> Mourning is regularly the reaction to the loss of a loved person, or to the loss of some abstraction which has taken the place of one, such as one's country, liberty, an ideal and so on. (p. 243)
>
> In analyses it often becomes evident that first one and then another memory is activated, and that the laments which always sound the same and are wearisome in their monotony nevertheless take their rise each time in some different unconscious source. (p. 256)

In my view, what gives racism its murderous quality are the deeper sources of the laments that need to be understood, which Powell's speech alludes to in terms of where these may be unconsciously located. Not only is the arrival of the foreigner felt to be a symbolic loss representing a loved person such as community, country, or nationhood, there is also a grievance that a betrayal has taken place, allowing the perceived influx of foreigners to contaminate an idealised relationship. This can manifest in notions of pure and ideal geographical territories, liberties, values, and customs.

Three years before Powell's speech, ITN News televised the first meeting of the British Ku Klux Klan at their Birmingham headquarters, who said of immigrants:

> [Britain is] being invaded by the silent black invasion which consists of the scum and the throw-outs of their stinking black countries. Our argument is not with the nigger in the street but the pigs who have brought them over here. (Larcourt, 1965)

I suggest that this grievance relates to an imaginary couple who have inflicted this loss for which revenge is sought. Racism becomes a battle with an imaginary couple, which is being played out on the stage of ethnicity. Social grievances become the battlegrounds—what is at stake is the sense of self. Whereas the shadow of the object falls on the ego in melancholia, in racism this shadow is projected onto the dark stranger. This takes us into a broader canvas of inquiry where the primal scene fantasy can provide a useful conceptual framework to understand the nature of the losses suffered and the motivation to seek a racist solution.

CHAPTER TWO

The racist scene and the primal scene

The racist scene

When I came to Britain in the 1970s, it was impossible to avoid the racist graffiti etched across the walls of the houses in our neighbourhood, which started to have an impact once I realised that the offensive words and imagery were aimed at foreigners like myself. Typical examples included graffiti slogans which demanded that "Pakis wogs go home", "you dirty fucking Pakis", complaints of food smells in the street, or excrement being posted through letter boxes of homes owned by people from Asian communities.

I suggest that racist events, wherever we may encounter them, have an unconscious narrative which I refer to as a "racist scene". It contains fantasies and feelings belonging to another scene altogether, which is largely unconscious. As outlined in the previous chapter, the structure of grievance in racism appears to involve elements of bewilderment, symbolic loss, powerlessness, betrayal, and a particular strategy of revenge. I propose that *thwarting the other* links the racist scene to the psychoanalytic notion of the "primal scene", in which complex psychic issues are being worked out. Like fantasies of the primal scene, racist scenes also involve an intermingling of benign and malignant elements that contain racial and racist fantasies respectively, oscillating between a sense of curiosity and concern that accommodates the ethnic other and descent into a spiral of hatred and revenge.

The primal scene

Freud (1918b) originally conceived of the primal scene as the child's perception or fantasy of his parents' love-making, which he interprets as an act of violence initiated by the father upon the mother—an idea that provokes sexual excitement and confusion in a child with limited mental capacity for processing these feelings. The term first appeared in his case of the "Wolf Man", demonstrating the theory of the Oedipus complex and his discovery of the infantile neurosis lying at its core. Preoccupied with determining whether the primal scene was a fantasy or an actual event that took place, his work on the sexual theories of children (1908c) reflects his emphasis on the child's fantasy interpretation of the scene, which he describes as "the sadistic theory of coitus" (p. 221).

Whether the primal scene is actually witnessed or fantasised, the nature of what is being psychically worked out at both pre-Oedipal and Oedipal levels of mental organisation form different referents for the primal scene. In other words, there are multi-layered psychic issues that are being worked out by the child when the two parents are brought together. McDougall (1980) conceptualised the scene in terms of the child's "total store of unconscious knowledge and personal mythology concerning the human sexual relation, particularly that of his parents" (p. 56). Thus, while sexuality is central to the primal scene, much more is being worked out here through the child's curiosity and imaginative reconstruction of the interaction and relationship between the parents, which Kohon (2012) describes as one of the compelling "enigmas of childhood". This perspective enables an appreciation of the multidimensional nature, quality, and function of primal scene fantasies as symbolised in the child's enigmatic perception, curiosity, understanding, and experience of the sexual. The primal scene is therefore not viewed as inherently traumatic or pathogenic but as a potentially constructive structure for organising mental life (Aron, 1995; Esman, 1973), in which reaction to the primal scene varies on a spectrum, from the destructively malignant to the more life-enhancing and benign.

In contrast to Freud, Klein conceptualised the malignancy of the primal scene in part-object terms, as a frightening amalgam in the child's mind in which the sexual organs of the parents are intertwined in violence, representing the most primitive version of the primal scene. The ensuing chaos is thought to arise because there is little differentiation in the elements that make up this frightening combined figure, which she termed the "combined-parent figure". The function of this monstrous figure is partly to deny the parental intercourse as well as a projection of hostility towards this relationship.

Whether the parental couple in the primal scene come together in a lively and pleasurable or destructive way is thought to have a profound effect on the capacity for thinking. Since thinking necessitates making links, it also forms the prototype for the development of creativity as symbolised by how the parental couple are linked together in the mind (Bion, 1962a; Meltzer, 1973). A capacity to link thoughts, to think, and to create meaning, is therefore shaped by the way the parents in the Oedipal situation are perceived and used, determining the shape of the mental space.

In this way a link has been made between the developmental tasks in the Oedipal situation and the way mental space is structured, affecting the capacity to comprehend and relate to reality. The development of curiosity and concern towards the other requires the recognition of the other as a fellow human being, separate from oneself—a recognition that comes out of a particular state of mind termed the depressive position (Klein, 1946). In contrast, the paranoid-schizoid mode of functioning mobilises splitting and projection to obstruct that recognition.

Ogden's (1989) work is an extension of thinking in this area and connects the paranoid-schizoid mode of being to the most malignant response, in which the child is caught up in the primal scene with a frightful sense of bewilderment, unable to make sense of the experience because of his or her limited capacity for observation or reflection. When the primal scene is experienced and perceived in the depressive mode of functioning, the child is more of a participant-observer, aware of him or herself as separate in relation to parents as whole objects. This can form the basis for the development of subjectivity and the parental couple to be experienced at an Oedipal level.

Britton (1989) refers to this development in mental life as the creation of a "triangular space", which introduces new challenges that provoke anxiety in the child's mind. If the anxieties of feeling excluded from the parental relations are manageable it introduces different possibilities, that of being an observer of the parents' relationship and allowing oneself to be observed in relation to another. This is dependent on the individual's capacity to play with different configurations of links between objects in the mind, which include the realisation of both the anatomical/sexual as well as generational differences that are present in the triangular situation between children and parents.

I suggest that curiosity about these links and what they give rise to determines whether mental space expands to accommodate knowledge about these "facts of life" or contracts if the anxiety is too intolerable. In this way the quality of thinking is linked to the degree of separateness achieved (Segal, 1957). Changes from two-dimensional to three-dimensional thinking, that reflects psychic complexity and diversity, will depend on the type of anxieties dominating the individual, group or organisation at any given moment. Central to these discoveries is a capacity to bear loss and mourning as part of the recognition of one's position in the larger scheme of things that psychic complexity brings forth. It is a lifelong struggle to learn and comprehend the complexity of this ordinary human reality, a development that is thought to bring about a different conception of mental space, and quality and depth to thinking and feeling.

The link between the primal and racist scene

These ideas are helpful in understanding the quality of thinking in racist states of mind that reflect a more malignant version of the primal scene in which the paranoid-schizoid mode of functioning is dominant, in contrast to the use of racial fantasies for exploring the other. Here, the development of a sense of curiosity and concern recognises separateness, characteristic of a more depressive mode of being that acknowledges feelings of loss and mourning. The malignant reaction, on the other hand, can involve uncontrollable feelings of rage and revenge as an expression of being narcissistically wounded by the sense of being excluded, rejected, and intruded upon by the parents' exclusive relationship. For example, in the racist scene of the playground where the Black teenager was attacked, there was, at first, White bewilderment at the sight of the black skin, with deeper questions in the unconscious minds of the White teenagers as to just who this black boy was, how and why he was there, and who was responsible for his presence.

In Britton's description of a patient who was unable to tolerate his capacity to think as an analyst, his patient shouted at him "stop that

THE RACIST SCENE AND THE PRIMAL SCENE 15

fucking thinking". His patient experienced and symbolically equated Britton's thinking to an act of sexual intercourse that could not be tolerated. It echoes my example of the racist graffiti, "you dirty fucking Paki", which expresses a certain discovery and recognition that is felt to be forced upon the perpetrator's mind of what is unremarkable: two people engaged in sexual intercourse.

Here, the arrival of the Black teenager in the playground may unconsciously represent a rival sibling who is attacked, but also an imaginary couple in the background who made this happen. This can extend to any configuration of couplings and productivity that is felt to rob the individual or nation, as Powell's speech demonstrates.

In contrast to this state of affairs, working through depressive functioning can potentially enable the couple in the mind to be allowed to come together to engage in a productive relationship where two contrasting ideas (gendered difference) can accommodate and interact with each other without becoming violated by fusion or splitting. This would be the emotional equivalent of sexual intercourse, in which different ideas can come together within the mind in the service of reflective and productive thinking or creativity and the capacity to manage contradiction and ambiguity (Feldman, 1989).

An example that comes to mind which speaks to the intermingling and oscillations of racial and racist fantasies at play is of a White male patient who spoke with fondness of his early experiences of living in colonial Africa and his exposure to the local Black "natives" in his neighbourhood. This was tinged with a sense of bewilderment about what kind of food they ate and his perception of their behaviour as dirty and unruly, which he found abhorrent. His next association to this was his Black neighbour in an apartment complex, whom he was convinced had made the carpet in the foyer dirty, without any evidence for his accusation except that, being from Africa, this was probably to be expected and all part of her normal behaviour. All this was spoken in an eminently reasonable tone, carrying with it a sign of his tolerance for other cultures, which barely hid his contempt. He then went on to tell me about how fascinated he had become with using foreign recipes in his cooking and that he found himself experimenting with all sorts of different combinations as if he was getting too carried away with it all and needed to reign himself in. I thought the patient experienced my attempts to understand him as "messing his mind up"— not unlike the reaction to his black neighbour or the experience of the

Black "natives"—but that he also felt that something productive was also happening, which was making him both excited and alarmed.

Thwarting the ethnic other in racism

In the context of the "rivers of blood" speech, we are in the realms of a more malignant state of affairs. The narrative touches on a different element of the primal scene in which the dominant theme is the imagined fear of a potent couple that will produce interlopers who will populate, contaminate, deplete, or rob the resources of the body or mind, group, or nation. Implicit in this fear are the pleasures derived from the erotic and gratifying links that the potent couple symbolise, from which the person feels excluded. These result in grievances stemming from hurts or injuries to the self that reflect many layers of betrayal and loss (notions of a community unblemished by immigrants, or the British Empire and Imperial superiority).

The unconscious attack on the symbolic potency of the couple in racism extends to any desire and ambition expressed by the new arrivals, such as, for example, the immigrant's wish to better his lot in life, to make a new home, and sustain himself from potential sources of nourishment; or pleasure expressed through his language, customs, community, and cultural life. The inherent pleasure each takes in their sense of "aliveness" or pleasure in their ethnic identity is too difficult to stomach for the racist, who is only consumed with loss and feels depleted or robbed, stirring up a wish for revenge.

This formulation has the potential of generating hypotheses about the type of defensive strategies employed in different contexts of racism in order to subvert the notion of a potent couple in the mind through oppressive socio-political arrangements. For example, in the context of South Africa, the working lives of Black domestic workers are often organised around the needs of their White employers, which increasingly cut across class lines and different ethnicities. In the past, under apartheid, this psychic splitting of the couple was institutionalised by the segregation laws which kept Black families apart, separated in the townships from the city and predominantly White neighbourhoods. It is how the dependency on Black workers is experienced and treated unconsciously that is interesting, such as the housemaid or mine worker whose enslavement involves both low wages and living away from their partners and families. This type of splitting appears to serve the purpose of not acknowledging fully how the privileged lives of their White employers was also made possible through the black maid's labour, or in the case of the mine worker, the commodity itself, such as the material object of mineral wealth.

Low wages ensure their dire economic circumstances keep them in permanent bondage and dependency through starving them of the most basic infrastructure. This created appalling living conditions that forced the poorest Blacks to experience deprivation, lack of family cohesion, and powerlessness. Keeping the townships to which they belonged geographically and psychically out of sight, and out of mind, also bolsters the delusion that it is the Blacks who are responsible for their deprived conditions and squalor and do not deserve anything better. This feeds into racist stereotypes that perceive Blacks as not capable of being responsible adults.

There is, however, a further dynamic at play: these oppressive arrangements also serve to displace White envy, which is more evident in its projected form, by getting Blacks to experience these painful feelings. Since envy seeks to spoil, devalue or misappropriate qualities of an object without recognition of their origin, it misrepresents the emotional significance of the object. Money-Kyrle's (1978) description of envy as a "robbery in imagination" comes close to how pleasures derived from erotic and gratifying links and their derivatives, symbolised by the couple, are triumphantly robbed in racism as it watches over the helpless, impotent, and envious state of mind it seeks to create in the ethnic other, who are now at the receiving end. Fanon (1967) captured this dynamic in his seminal work "The Wretched of the Earth".

> ... the look that the native turns on the settler's town is a look of lust, a look of envy; it expresses his dreams of possession—all manner of possession: to sit at the settler's table, to sleep in the settler's bed, with his wife if possible. The colonized man is an envious man. And this the settler knows very well; when their glances meet he ascertains bitterly, always on the defensive, "They want to take our place." It is true, for there is no native who does not dream at least once a day of setting himself up in the settler's place. (p. 30)

Racist states of mind: a formulation

The primary drivers in racist states of mind appear to be grievances unconsciously based on the narcissistic injury of witnessing and feeling excluded or marginalised from an object engaged in a good or potent experience, a coupling within a primal scene scenario. This grievance contains bewilderment, powerlessness, perceived betrayal, feelings of loss, and a wish for revenge, which is achieved primarily through thwarting the potency of ethnic others. An expression of desire, a liveliness, and life-affirming hunger becomes a phobic object which is envied, feared, despised, and attacked because this experience is felt as a contamination that has to be cleaned up or purified by expelling this dangerous other from the psyche.

It is often expressed as a nostalgic reverie that has become stuck and yearns for a return to an imagined and idealised state free from intrusions, such as the minor differences that ethnicity brings forth. It forces a recognition of both sexual and generational differences as the basis of diversity that is encapsulated in the Oedipal situation. These painful feelings of real or imagined loss and the necessity of mourning is sidestepped and managed through a retreat into omnipotence and manic mechanisms that offer the additional excitement of hatred and violence.

Thus, temporary relief of this internal state is achieved through traumatising the ethnic other by attacking and attempting to dismantle significant links or connections to their good or potent objects and throwing their sense of self into profound doubt. What is attacked includes the sense of feeling secure and comfortable in one's physical and psychic skin and the symbolic equivalent in the world of language, culture, and customs that make up a personal and cultural identity. A racist state of mind attempts to tear these links apart to create a dislocation from inner objects which normally serve as potential resources to the self, group, or society and, in this way, aims to get those on the receiving end to experience trauma and loss.

PART II

RACE IN THE CONSULTING ROOM

CHAPTER THREE

Working clinically with racist states of mind

This chapter looks more closely at what are essentially identity struggles that are acted-out on the stage of ethnicity through preoccupations about ethnicity, race, or racism in the clinical situation. Calvo's (2008) work suggests that the central anxiety in racist hatred is both a fear and desire of mixing or miscegenation, experienced in the most primitive layers of the mind as a violent contamination. It calls upon what he terms "racial fantasy structures" in his analysis of how the anxiety of mixing blood and races, central to miscegenation, links to an existing anxiety about sexuality and sexual difference. Racial fantasy structures are thought to organise one's relations to the other through encounters with difference. Like all primal scene fantasies, these structures are concerned with fundamental questions about the relationship between self and other, or questions about one's origin (Laplanche & Pontalis, 1986). I would add that central to these psychic discoveries is the inevitable pain of loss and mourning as essential vehicles for moving the psyche forward that are strongly resisted in a racist state of mind.

The racist scene, as I have suggested, is a variant of the primal scene fantasy where the structure of racial fantasies reflect an intense preoccupation with the other in its ethnic or racial form. These deep structures of thought and feeling are universally present in various hidden forms in contemporary culture as well as the consulting room, where they may come to constitute the passions of the transference. Here the therapist's ethnic or racial difference provides a medium to bring fresh life to early experiences and give particular shape and form to the transference. It opens up a distinction that I suggest needs to be made between the use of *racial* and *racist* fantasies, whose functions are different; the former notices the ethnic characteristics of others and is motivated by a curiosity that can signal a wish to explore the self in relation to others. In contrast are racist fantasies that aim to thwart and damage others, closing down any possibilities of intimacy with and learning from others about the self. It links directly with the argument that the racist scene is a refraction of the primal scene fantasy, the unconscious functions of which are varied. In the example of the patient who began to explore his relationship to food and cooking, both racial and racist fantasies were "cooking" in his unconscious, linking up with his past through his experience with me, which introduced the possibility of learning about himself.

Thoughts and feelings about the ethnic other can weave between a sense of curiosity and a structure of thought and feeling that reflects a wish for absolute certainty. One configuration of this internal situation is a defensive or narcissistic organisation in the mind that Rosenfeld (1971) has called a "psychic gang", an amalgam of attitudes which creates an ambience of brutality, with omnipotence, arrogance, cruelty, thuggery, and violence as part of its working. These are brought into play to ward off anxieties that are varied in nature, but which relate to change, growth, and development of the self.

Intolerance is a striking feature in this organisation, which claims absolute certainty in relation to another—be it a person, belief, or ideology. In doing so it becomes more like a colonisation, the sole possession of a claim to truth that reflects a violation of boundaries between self and other. This violation undermines that capacity for self-observation which enables us to take up different positions in relation to others and creates the possibilities for empathy and concern.

The colonised space is rigid and narrow, in contrast to a more fluid space with possibilities. This narrow-mindedness is also expressed in totalitarian thinking, which permits only one opinion, as in one party politics, with no room for rival thoughts and feelings that might express differences of any kind. The passion involved in this possession often conveys an internal fortress-like structure, rigid and impermeable to any other possibility of thought or feeling. A mental organisation of this type is essentially a paranoid one, difficult to access through reason or judgment and, because of a failure in the capacity to comprehend reality, there is a constant pull towards putting the brakes on psychic growth and development.

In this mental organisation, differences that are perceived from the outside as fundamental to growth and development, and of life itself, are experienced internally as undermining the stability it seeks to create. Large parts of the outside world are closed down through subjugation of the space for curiosity, imagination, and learning from, and concern for, others. Within a psychoanalytic understanding, what is destroyed are links or relationships to the good object embodied in maternal dependency and its extension into parental sexuality and relations. It includes an attack on the very links that comprise knowledge about these facts of life and the inevitable consequences for separation, loss, growth, and development. The capacity to obstruct or pervert a knowing that a development of curiosity and concern might bring forth creates a fraudulent state of affairs that takes precedence over an awareness of the real complexities of life and living.

The clinical situation

In the clinical situation, as in the world at large, concrete features such as skin colour or ethnicity are sometimes used as an opportunistic vehicle by the patient to project the intolerable feelings that a different viewpoint might engender. In this way, the therapist becomes the hook on which to hang psychic material that the patient finds too difficult to think about. The purpose of this projective process is varied at any given moment in the session. It can be in the service of communicating what is unbearable and cannot be put into words, so that the therapist is used like a temporary container for what the fragile psyche cannot hold.

Sometimes he can be used like a dustbin, a psychic toilet to evacuate the contents of their mind, or at other moments it is a means of controlling the therapist in a sadistic way. In contrast to these states is sometimes an increased capacity to think and reflect, pointing to the development of a broader state of mind. The reality of clinical work is that often a combination of all these motives are present and have to be understood and worked with from moment to moment.

Developmentally, the skin can serve the purpose of providing the most basic type of holding or containment (Bick, 1968; Anzieu, 1970;

Ogden, 1989). It serves to bind the most primitive parts of the personality in the earliest stages of life through the experience of being contained by the skin of the other, to eventually introject this function and enable one to experience the feeling of being contained in one's own "psychological skin". The therapist's unwelcome intrusion in the form of interpretations or actions such as changes in timing of sessions or breaks can often stir up primitive or psychotic anxieties that can be racialised (Keval, 2001). The magnitude of the anxiety can be expressed through violent means, sometimes as an act of desperation, using the only medium of communication available to the patient.

Alternatively, at a less primitive level, we could understand the patient's attacks more as a wish for revenge for a narcissistic injury arising from the wounding recognition that the therapist is a separate person, the knowledge of which constitutes an insult (Gabbard, 1993); or, indeed, a recognition that exposes the patient and sometimes leads to feelings of shame and humiliation. This recognition can then be retaliated against by attempts to force the therapist to experience the same feelings. Because reactions to narcissistic wounds are different from the sense that the psychic skin is no longer functioning, it necessitates listening to the kinds of fantasies, anxieties, and defences attached to these experiences. These may be in the realm of chaos and un-integration, a failure of basic skin-holding, disintegration, and persecutory states, characteristic of the paranoid-schizoid position, or curiosity and concern of the depressive position. None of these states are absolute and fixed, but remain fluid so that there is constant movement from one to the other with variations between individuals in terms of which end of the spectrum their mental life is predominantly located at any given moment.

One of the most difficult tasks for the therapist is how to help the patient take ownership of their racist projections and to assist them in metabolising or integrating them within their psyche so that reparative processes can be potentially set in motion. This involves understanding grievances from past and present relationships in the patient's life that are displaced onto ethnic others. Both infantile and adult concerns are implicated in racist states of mind. Working through these difficulties involves the arduous task of giving up grievances and taking responsibility for destructiveness to others and to the self, and confronting the painful feelings of shame and guilt that this can bring about. Combined with the loss of loyalty to the racist organisation, this can come to feel potentially unbearable. However, if grief and mourning are allowed to proceed then a possibility arises for the patient to make reparation and live a less destructive, and self-destructive, life.

One of the obstacles to effective working through is the lure of manic and omnipotent states, where more racial intolerance is unleashed, creating further spirals of guilt. Reactive defences are brought into play to triumph over feelings of despair that have to be constantly eliminated through further projections into ethnic others. This traps both victim and perpetrator alike into a toxic cycle. Whether these states erupt in a bombastic way or in extremely subtle and silent ways, the difficult therapeutic task is how to remain robust and empathic in the face of the patient's brutality so that a language can be found to speak to the patient's predicament. This is a difficult undertaking given that these states of mind contain a strong presence of thuggery and violence which are used to resist psychic pain. The therapist has to resist pressures to feel either defeated or to gratify his sadistic impulses of wishing to triumph over the patient (Carpy, 1989). Striving to think and understand while under fire is an attempt to act as a container that survives for the patient in the hope that he or she can gradually feel strong enough to resist turning to a racist solution for their difficulties.

As I have mentioned, an organisation of this type can sometimes appear in the patient's material as different parts of the personality, where the most vulnerable part of the patient is trying to keep sane but is easily led by a more destructive aspect with which there is an unconscious alliance. This can disguise the fraudulent element of the scenario in which the patient often finds the excitement of the destructiveness irresistible. As one of my patients said, he was a "willing accomplice" in the pleasure derived from wreaking havoc on his life.

In these situations the therapist is invited or forced to observe and experience a combination of both enthrallment and helplessness in the patient that is idealised in a chilling way. Sometimes the patient is quite aware and insightful about his situation but appears powerless to do anything about it, despite desperate attempts to let the therapist become aware of his predicament.

Steiner (1982) suggests that this phenomenon may be understood in terms of a continuum in the degree of malignancy of the narcissistic organisation, particularly the idea that both the healthy and destructive parts of the personality contain both good and bad aspects, disguising the nature of the more destructive part and allowing perverse elements

to be associated with the healthy parts. This creates a perverse relationship between the two parts of the self where the healthy dependent
self is all too willing to become a victim. Both therapist and patient can
be perceived (depending on whose experience it is) as making it intolerable to have a space to think without undermining or negating the
other. Floundering in this type of noxious atmosphere, the therapist can
be perceived as peddling a belief that is equally, if not more unhelpful
than the one held by the patient.

This malignant dependency is often expressed in the way the mental space is structured, such that there is very little movement or room
for fluidity in the patient's mind—an experience that the clinician is
often invited or forced to experience. The most familiar presentation
is when the brutal attitude of the patient in relation to his own vulnerability is enacted in the transference so that the therapist is experienced
as a rather pathetic, needy figure who is treated brutally. The therapist's
desire and commitment to help in these circumstances may be like a red
rag to a bull, intensifying the patient's contempt.

In one of my patients, his addiction to pornography revealed,
amongst other things, his utter contempt for feelings to do with care
or tenderness, which he associated with passivity and femininity. In
his conscious and unconscious racism towards Blacks it was also evident that he equated them with the same contempt he had for women,
whom he found desirable and needing to be brought under his control through sexual exploitation in one way or another. He would often
make comments enquiring about his obsession with sexual excitement
that involved a fantasy of obliteration or annihilating his partners.
In this way, he believed he could obliterate the object in himself that
contained feelings of vulnerability that he found intolerable. Recount-
ing these fantasies revealed his addiction, excitement, and desperation,
but also a small hint of a growing capacity for curiosity about his inner
state. The latter could easily be crushed when he became arrogant and
contemptuous of the fact that I (or anybody else for that matter) could
continue to have the desire to help him in a humane way.

When the patient's tentative steps to become more curious, imaginative, and concerned about his object or himself creates too much
anxiety, some patients will retreat into a racist state of mind that
aims to temporarily hijack or, more seriously, crush their momentary
growth and development. At these times there is little if no room for
a third position, a different viewpoint, or a new perspective, as this

would be experienced as "stepping out of line"—the therapist having an independent mind that is beyond the reach of the patient's wish for control. This interpersonal situation throws light on how racism organises itself, both internally and in the external world, by keeping its needed objects denigrated and given prescribed roles so that the racist dictum is kept in force: "Know your place". The corollary of the ethical imperative is the implied threat: "and do not cause trouble by stepping out of line".

This of course creates therapeutic challenges in working clinically with the cunning face of cruelty and control in racism. The complexity of the various alliances and collusions in the defensive organisation of the patient's mind necessitates the need for the therapist to be independent, while recognising that it is this very function that enrages the patient because the therapist is "stepping out of line" and threatening the racist organisation.

Whether understanding is enough to render the potency of this organisation less influential in its functioning is an interesting question, especially with some patients who will blatantly tell you that such an understanding is all very well and good but it does nothing to change their behaviour. Closer analysis, however, usually reveals how the understanding itself is brutalised so that its potency has been stripped of meaning and potential helpfulness.

The following case studies attempt to speak to some of these themes and predicaments in the consulting room for both patient and therapist. Several themes emerge in these analyses. Ethnic differences between the patient and myself were used as a psychic pathway to manage anxiety or pain in an opportunistic way that echoes how the dynamics of racism operate in the external world. This is most evident in the way the theme of "stepping out of line" emerges when the patient could not tolerate my behaving with an independent mind, rather than being subservient. It was also evident in their own struggle to develop the courage to think independently in the face of a loyalty to denigrating ethnic others, thwarting the analytic process and themselves. Key to their childhood histories were weaknesses or failures in triangulating that had implications for the kind of mental space and relations they inhabited when under the grip of this type of thinking.

Helping patients to metabolise their guilt from racist projections can be challenging for the therapist because of the risks of becoming caught up with the patient's internal culture of brutality, but reparative attempts can lead to a more humane attitude of the patient towards himself and others.

Patient B[1]

Ms. B was a White woman in her thirties who came to see me for help with her panic attacks. She said she was both intimidated and fascinated by the prospect of coming to see me in an outpatient clinic in an area which she imagined was typically middle-class, as opposed to the more impoverished area in which she grew up.

In one session she was preoccupied with this contrast by describing the area in which she lived as "scum" compared to an adjacent, more affluent area in which she spent long periods playing as a child. She began to tell me how this area was associated with people who were clearly better off in all sorts of ways, namely wealth, access to books, music, knowledge about the world, and having the luxury to travel and discover foreign places. In short, everything she wanted for herself but was unable to achieve, seeing her mother's narrow-mindedness as the main obstacle to these opportunities.

She thought the "scum" area in which she lived was racist and associated this with her mother and sister, who could not stand the sight of Blacks, Asians, or foreigners in general. She was told that if she ever brought a Black man home she would be kicked out of the house. She did not think of herself as racist because she had Asian and Black friends, whom she would openly call "Pakis", but she did not see that as being racist as she liked being with them. Some of her White friends reminded her that calling them "Pakis" was hardly a sign of tolerance. She was, however, adamant that it was her mother and sister who denigrated Asian and Black people. Rather sheepishly, she would tell me that she occasionally joined in the racist conversations that frequently took place in their home.

It was clear that, as much as she desired my company, she could not stand the sight of my brown face. The therapeutic task was how to help her understand what lay behind her panic. Understanding and managing her own intolerance and narrow-mindedness, projected into her mother as the vehicle, was clearly part and parcel of this task. My therapeutic leverage was her sense of fascination with all sorts of differences and possibilities that she could not as yet accommodate in her mind. This was the play-area of her childhood and her infantile self that she mentioned was being robbed by her mother.

On hearing her rather fast-paced account, I was struck by just how action-orientated her use of words such as "scum", "kicked out", "Pakis", and so on were, suggesting that the patient was inhabiting a world of concrete thinking where anxieties were being acted-out with words to evacuate distress. I found myself feeling both rattled and bemused by the apparent ease with which she seemed to be telling me this without any embarrassment or shame, nor any concern of how this Asian man in front of her would experience her barrage of comments. This became clearer when she told me that her Asian friends would go along with her behaviour, laughing it all off. Yet she also recognised that she could not defend her Black friends in conversations when her mother and others were being offensive. While Ms. B was telling me that she felt powerless to think for herself in the face of a cruel object that she located in her mother, her demeanour in the session told me that her collusion had much to do with her own gratification from this type of cruelty.

Interactions like these suggest a number of different possibilities and avenues for understanding and interpretation. The two geographical areas represented two aspects of herself, a couple at war with each other: one harbouring an attitude of cruelty and superiority through her racism, and another, vulnerable, but also thoughtful and potentially curious—a part of herself that both fascinated and frightened her.

When she spoke of her mother being an obstacle to the opportunities available to her, she was referring to her own propensity to thwart her life through her racist hatred—a proclivity she also identified in her mother, from whom she found it difficult to separate. Her bondage to racist hatred concealed her hatred of triangulation, where Blacks or foreigners represented her hidden desire to connect to a much-needed third object, her father, whom she had lost in her adolescence when he died from an illness. This relationship could have paved a potential gateway into a world of diversity, a journey that could have enabled her to become a woman with her own mind and a life of her own, rather than remain in a sadomasochistic relationship with her mother.

My task was to help her understand how and why she was obstructing this developmental journey, which had to do with recognising the painful fact that, what she perceived to be an external obstruction, her racist mother, her own racist attitudes were what was hindering her development, conveniently projected into her mother and therefore unavailable for scrutiny and change. When I put these thoughts to her she became dismissive. I was in a quandary about how to speak to her lack of concern in this attitude without sounding as if I was judging or punishing her. The risk was of closing down inquiry and exploration and getting drawn into a false type of certainty that would only have reinforced an internal sadomasochistic situation. Perhaps my anxiety that I would tell her off for being dismissive reflected the cruelty of her inner world where a harsh superego would castigate her and stop the development of any further thinking between us.

In moments like these, the therapist can get drawn in to acting like a thug, stopping the patient from being racist, reflecting the very thug she had identified as obstructing her life—a thug that she projected into her mother. Stopping the thug would have provided some comfort for me in not having to listen to her attitudes, but it would have only repeated and enacted the object relationship, pushing it underground, unavailable for closer scrutiny and understanding. What needed to be found was the possibility of speaking to her apparent lack of concern in her racist attitude in a way that would have invited her to think with me.

My temporary inability to do this in that moment reflected my anxiety of becoming a thug who could exact revenge on her, out of not wanting to hear any more racist remarks. It tells us something important about how easy it is to get caught up in the patient's inner world of cruelty and narrow-mindedness, where only black-and-white thinking exists.

Regardless of her initial reaction to my interpretation, what was important was not to collude with her racist attitude without question, as she described her Asian friends doing. To bypass it was to miss an important opportunity for exploring her own fear of standing up to her racist attitudes that took grip of her capacity to be more thoughtful.

In the following session, she said she was puzzled by how upset she had become after she left me, as she always thought it was her mother and sister who were racist, whereas she sometimes tried to defend her Asian and Black friends. I thought she had recovered a capacity to feel humane again, trying to reconcile her racist feelings with concern for the very person she had come to for help. Ms. B was clearly struggling to metabolise an unpalatable aspect of her own functioning that she habitually projected into her mother. Her upset was then replaced with laughter and denial as she insisted that she was not being racist but just picking up on certain characteristics of cultures.

She used the fact that her Asian or Black friends were not immune to racist thinking as leverage in the session to cope with a painful acknowledgement of her own projection, as well as testing me to see whether I, like her Asian friends, would also collude by evading these difficult feelings between us. She maintained that it was a joke, just like her mother and sister would joke, but she recognised that she felt pressured to take their side and found it difficult to defend her Asian friends. I put it to her that she had come to see me to discover her own point of view in relation to others, such as her mother, sister, or with me, without feeling that she had to take sides. She replied thoughtfully that it was not just racism, it was anything different, like ideas, places, or people that her mother and sister hated because they were used to the same old ways of doing things, whereas she wanted to try things that were different. I suggested to her that she located in her mother and sister the old ways of thinking and feeling, which she was struggling to take responsibility for in herself. Her racism stopped her from thinking and becoming more curious about her own feelings and thoughts as a separate person, and different from her mother, because it made her feel terribly anxious.

Ms. B replied that wanting to think differently made her feel afraid and then told me about a teacher on a course she was attending whom she found very knowledgeable, but if she was to be seen talking to her in the street she would die of embarrassment because of her association with her. She thought this teacher belonged to a group of people who were dirty scroungers on child benefits. She said she felt terrible in the way she was so two-faced about this. I put to her that she found herself with feelings that were more complicated than the black-and-white thinking and feeling she preferred, such as feeling embarrassed about needing help from me, like the teacher she admired. She looked upset and said she often lacked the courage to speak out against her racist feelings.

She then spoke about her Spanish boyfriend who boasted that, unlike the British, he came from a race that was pure and uncontaminated by foreigners. This conversation became all the more difficult for her when her mother responded to his comments by saying that these foreigners were not British at all. She tried to challenge her mother that some of her Black friends were indeed British because they were born in this country, but she began to feel alone in her thinking.

I suggested to her that I thought there were moments when she felt more able to speak her mind with her mother and members of her family and other moments when she felt very alone and frightened to speak up, which made her want to run back into what was familiar to her, namely the comfort of her racist thinking. She replied that it was too dangerous to speak out, as she witnessed the consequences of doing this when her boyfriend was beaten up for being Spanish by thugs who were her own relatives.

Overview

It is interesting how this woman's adolescent struggle for identity is expressed through her preoccupations about racism. Her claim of being more tolerant and liberal, in contrast to her mother and sister, was an attempt to punctuate a difference between herself and the "older" generation of adults, an attempt at separation that failed her. Her choice of a foreign boyfriend also seemed to be an attempt to embrace difference, widening the aperture of her object relationships from her mother into a more Oedipal or triangular situation that reflected her genuine excitement and curiosity about the outside world. She was out to convince herself and others of her supposed tolerance and that she was indeed a grown-up, ready to enter the adult world. This was the more healthy part of her which wished to move away from the narrow confines of the pure "uncontaminated space" in which only she and her mother resided, an imagined space free of foreign experiences of all kinds, including the world of her much-needed father.

Unfortunately, this separation was fraught with difficulties as she found herself in a relationship with a man who also idealised racist beliefs. Thus her attempt to flee from an internal racist object landed her in another relationship with a man who echoed the racist sentiments of her mother. The patient's internal predicament was of wanting to remain loyal to a part of herself in bondage to a racist object that despised any growth and development, while at the same time wishing to forge a separate space and identity. However, challenging this object by challenging racist sentiments brought profound anxieties in relation to potential threats of violence and banishment into a place where she felt utterly alone, without the internal resources to sustain her, urging her to run back to her objects of safety. The process was all the more difficult for her in the absence of a father, who could have potentially helped her in this transition. While opportunities to explore her early life in more depth were limited, this racialised crisis around separation and loss may have echoed earlier infantile crises that her adolescence had brought to the surface again (Blos, 1962).

The struggle for emotional freedom in Ms. B had another opportunity of being worked at in the transference with me, where our conspicuous racial differences brought fresh life to this internal conflict. One can see how these developmental struggles took on a more ominous tone when they became entrenched in the form of a racist object relationship which used thuggery to wreak violence if any attempt was made to achieve separation or acknowledge ordinary ambivalence. In contrast, I represented an object that could think with her and foster her own independence of mind, but this required acknowledging that she needed me, which was the sticking point. The reality of her dependency on me was hidden behind her sense of racist superiority, which it was too psychically dangerous to speak out against. Given her history, these dangers would have included the terrors associated with the risks of becoming dependent on me as someone who was the subject of contempt and murderous impulses, which aligned me with a father who died (psychically murdered/killed off) at a crucial stage in her development.

To not challenge and explore her attitudes would have risked leaving intact her inner racist arrangement, which would have left her at the mercy of the brutality of her racism, which pushed away any acknowledgement of more humane feelings to do with her own needs. She projected her infantile self into her Spanish boyfriend's weaker grasp of the English language and the darker-skinned complexion of her Asian friends and therapist, creating unconscious avenues for locating any kind of weakness or vulnerability. Her contempt for, and projection of her infantile self was clear when she described her teacher as dirty and needy, but this defensive strategy protected her from the reality of a real need for help in separating from her infantile introjects and entering young womanhood—a development that necessitated the work of mourning. Her racist state of mind was brought into play through a number of opportune moments that gave her a sense of superiority through her denigration of others. Her wish for everything to be black-and-white was a plea for simplicity in the face of the real complexity of her identifications between her mother and father, derivatives of a primitive conflict between love and hate that made use of a racist template to make her life more manageable.

This solution attempted to carve out a degree of separation by fleeing from an internal object and seeking refuge in an external one, in this case her foreign boyfriend, only to find herself at the mercy of both his racism and her own. The cost was the loss of a sense of reality.

In the transference she could idealise me as knowledgeable, like her teacher, but rendered unbearable as I was also denigrated. The reality was that she could not tolerate the shame and embarrassment of needing my help, attempting to recruit me into her racist thinking by turning the whole matter into a joke, inviting me to collude with her so that her hidden loyalties to the racist object remained intact. To come clean with her feelings about her Black or Asian friends would have been tantamount to betraying her loyalty to the racist organisation that she had signed up to. Being two-faced meant she could declare her loyalty to her racism, but only secretly declare her more humane or tender feelings for me and her teacher on whom she was dependent for help. Being two-faced also meant she could escape punishment by the "thugs" in her mind who could not tolerate any acknowledgement of difference or separateness and therefore any possibility of growth and development. This retreat ensured that she remained sealed-off from the "posh" world of her father, a world of curiosity, discovery, and learning that she was so keen to embrace, but also required her to recognise the significance of her father, which would have completed the Oedipal triangle.

However, by keeping the internal couple warring in her mind, thoughts representing these objects could not come together either, so that links in her thinking could not be formed, sustained, or enjoyed, restricting her curiosity and capacity to think. The movements she made in her thinking, which showed some recognition of the error of her ways, suggested a small but growing capacity to tolerate the anxieties of the depressive position before it became hijacked.

The other consequence of keeping the Oedipal triangle incomplete was to leave her prey to racist thinking without an internal ally, such as an identification with a strong father who could have helped her to have the courage to speak her mind instead of giving in to an attitude of cruelty and hatred towards herself and others who were different. It is an interesting question as to whether she would have been able to be more independent if he had held the same racist beliefs as her mother.

Patient C

A White woman in her late forties, suffering from a long standing depression, spoke of her early experience growing up in Africa. She became very attached to her Black housemaid but saw her as second-best because she was not her real White mother, who was always busy in her various charitable projects.

One of the things I was struck by in her manner of talking was her ability to pick up mistakes I would occasionally make in my pronunciation which she would try to correct with an air of reasonableness about her, which veiled her contempt for me.

The main themes I will focus on appeared in a sequence of sessions when she was thinking about increasing her sessions from four to five times a week. This occurred in the context of her feelings about my impending summer break which were evident in the material of her dream the week before in which she was screaming at having had to wait in a queue to see me. She alluded to the feeling of being rejected by a couple whom she was friendly with and who now had a new child to which much of their attention was directed.

At the beginning of the week I had to reschedule one of her sessions to a later time in the day; she agreed, but told me when she arrived that she was simmering with rage. While she said she felt grateful that I managed to see her at a different time, what bothered her was that she could get so upset about it. She dreamt the night before that she had collapsed in a heap but then her bigoted neighbour (she had brought material in the past about this racist neighbour) came over the fence and lifted her up. She associated this neighbour with my trying to accommodate her with a different time for her session, "lifting" her mood and giving her support in this way, but of course this was little comfort to the screaming baby inside her that was not allowing this matter to be put to rest.

I thought she experienced this disruption as the actions of somebody preoccupied with their own concerns rather than her wellbeing, leaving her "fobbed-off" and wounded. Her rage was a sign that she was waking up to her own needs, and it shocked her that I was becoming more significant in her psychic life. This awareness was felt to be deeply insulting, as her analysis had taken an unexpected turn towards the discovery of a psychic truth that her brown-skinned therapist/maid had started to become important to her. However, I had effectively stepped out of line from my assigned role as a subservient maid in her inner world. In order to cope with this injury, she joined forces in her mind with an intolerant object, in the form of the racist neighbour, who hated me stepping out of line. She recruited this racist part of herself which "lifted her mood" and gave her some comfort in her sense of superiority that now emerged as a response to her need for me.

This formulation was further confirmed in the following session when she told me that she had been promoted to a more senior status in her job, pairing her with her senior colleague to comment on her junior colleagues' work performance. The mood was distinctly aimed at "blowing her own trumpet" and feeling competent at the expense of her junior colleagues' vulnerability. I made a comment about this in the context of what had been happening between us in the previous session, of how she felt so wounded by my moving her to a later time in the day. She said she felt shocked that she could be misusing her colleague's vulnerability in this way to bolster her own feelings of competence.

This paved a way towards further thoughts that her charitable mother misused the vulnerability of others to feel superior. I then elaborated on what I had said to her in the previous session—that she had indeed felt insulted by an increased awareness in herself about needing my help. The way she coped with this was by joining forces with that part of herself, like the bigoted neighbour and her mother with her charitable works, trying to diminish and cut me down to size. I was her much-needed but denigrated housemaid who had stepped out of line by making a decision independent of her, beyond my status, so to speak.

Ms. C replied that she was very shocked by what seemed to her was her prejudice towards me and wondered whether she always saw me as inferior from the moment of entering treatment with me. She had spoken in the past of an eminent White analyst whom she wanted to see, someone befitting her status, rather than what she insinuated was the second-class option, namely myself. She said she could not cope with thinking about this as she had spent all her life despising and distancing herself from her mother's bigotry, which lay behind the public persona of helping others in need.

It was clearly a painful and important discovery for her when she said she that was deeply upset and ashamed at mirroring her mother's behaviour, which she thought she had distanced herself from.

In the following session she said she had been thinking about our previous meeting and recalled how her mother would try to feel superior by trying to correct everything her housemaid would say, as the latter could not speak English very well. Similarly, she had been thinking about how she too would try and correct my pronunciation, suggesting a similar attitude towards me. She felt sorry for the way that she had been treating me and asked how long I had been aware of her behaviour. The tone of this question made me feel slightly suspicious, as I felt it was loaded, but I was unsure as to where this was going. However, in my own private reflection, I wondered whether I had subtly communicated to her that I had been hurt by her behaviour. Had she picked this up perhaps in the tone of my voice and was now trying to protect me out of concern? Or did she feel I might retaliate in some way that could compromise her emotional safety with me?

I thought my uneasiness had to do with a feeling that she may be using this moment to determine my weakness so that she could re-establish the fact that she was in charge once again, following the rupture of her defences in the previous sessions. Given what I knew about her feelings of being excluded, which she had alluded to in relation to her friends who had a new baby, it was possible that if I had known about her manner of relating to me and had not shared it with her she would have felt excluded from this knowledge that resided in my mind, something she had no access to. I silently wondered how much she was genuinely concerned about her superior attitude towards me, and therefore risking the pain of her guilt, or attempting to size-up the opposition, so to speak. In other words, there was a possibility that it was not so much the content of what I had said that she was interested in grappling with but the very fact that I should have the audacity, as her brown therapist/housemaid, to point something out to her that was so unpalatable.

When I took a moment to tell her that I was thinking about her question, she said she felt confused and that thinking about her prejudice had shocked her. She said she had noticed a change in herself and had been thinking about increasing her weekly sessions to get her "analysis sorted out". It was an interesting turn of phrase. At this moment in the session the confusion she felt was that she was trying to accommodate an unpalatable thought about herself that she had been accustomed to projecting into an internal object representing her intolerant mother. "Sorting it out" was a manic salvage operation to help her recover from the shock of acknowledging her racism, which did not sit comfortably with her self-perception as a progressive, White, liberal person. This might suggest that her wish to increase her sessions was to increase her vigilance to keep a closer eye on me. By making interpretations that shocked her, I was "stepping out of line" in my assigned role. This solution would be in contrast to another possibility in which motivation for increasing her sessions arose out of guilt about her treatment of me leading to a wish for manic repair to ensure I was not too damaged by her racist behaviour.

The very fact that we could both struggle to understand her behaviour also suggests that the patient felt an element of hope; that she could risk further exposure of herself in more frequent sessions because she had gained evidence that an unpalatable aspect of her functioning could be grappled with, survived by both of us, and understood.

A dream she recounted further illuminated some of these psychic manoeuvres. In this dream were a number of empty plastic containers while she was walking alongside a staircase that took her towards the top of a tower. She gave these empty containers to a little girl. Once she reached the top she could see different perspectives of the horizon and landscape which she found exciting. She then walked down the staircase towards the ground and described what she saw as the "land of plenty"—full of rich olive trees, oranges, and fruits ripe for picking. Her immediate associations to this dream were about the ivory-tower world of intellectual ideas, which she felt very excited about, as well as the interest and pride she took in her charitable activities.

The general mood or ambience of the dream seemed rather grand in nature, as if from the tall and empty refuge of her tower she owned everything down below, which excited her. She looked at the food/ analysis on the ground, rich for the picking but out of emotional connection and reach because of her superior attitude that led to starving herself (giving empty containers to the little girl). I had a feeling that there was a change of heart when she decided to come down the staircase, perhaps to eat real food/analysis, in her wish to increase her sessions. However, I was put in my place when she told me that she was off to Paris when I returned from my break. As she left the consulting room, I was preoccupied with an image of the Eiffel Tower in my mind.

Overview

Taking this patient's early history, her grievance about being placed in the hands of a Black maid while her mother was involved in charitable activities translated into a wish that demanded she be given a real mother in the form of a White analyst, anything else being second-best. The determination to keep me second-best in her psychic life, like her much-needed but despised maid, served a number of functions. It allowed her to create a split in her mind between an ideal mother (White) she longed to have versus a second-best housemaid (Black) who could, of course, never replace her mother but to whom she had become deeply attached. This maid represented her much-needed and denigrated object which she opportunistically projected into me, her brown-skinned therapist who could not be the ideal White analyst that she desired. This gave her a way to maintain a grievance which would be challenged if she were to value my help and accept that she was keeping herself emotionally starved and empty, like the containers on the staircase of her ivory tower.

Her narcissistic superiority, in the form of the intellectual world of the ivory tower, looking down on ordinary feelings to do with her real deprivation and need, took on a racist construction. She utilised our ethnic differences opportunistically to create a split in which I was to remain denigrated and therefore could not possibly offer anything of value to her. In this way, her mourning of her real loss could be concealed and replaced by a demand that anything offered to her would never be good enough.

Patient D

A White woman in her twenties experienced severe bouts of depression that were precipitated when she ended relationships with her boyfriends. She was fleetingly aware of her capacity to destroy her intimate relations with men when she started to get too close to them but seemed determined unconsciously to repeat this problem rather than grapple with it. In one of her relationships she terminated a pregnancy before ending the relationship. It was an ominous sign that nothing much was ever allowed to grow in her life. The interesting thing was that all her partners were Black, including the most recent man, with whom she worked. She was understandably worried that this relationship was going to meet the same fate, which gave her enough concern to bring her to the consultation and engage in further therapy.

I learnt that she came from a family with a very disturbed mother who became hysterical and controlling of all the family members, often in a very cruel way, which she said they all witnessed and endured. She felt her father encouraged them to tip-toe around her mother's moods, which underplayed the serious nature of her problems. This was often repeated with me when I found myself under pressure to skirt around her controlling behaviour as I imagine she might have felt in relation to her mother.

In our first meeting it quickly became apparent just how anxious she was under the thin veneer of appearing to be in charge and wanting to be in full control of our meeting. She forewarned me that she could be a "hard bitch". I came to understand this as her attitude of superiority and contempt towards anybody and anything to do with feelings of weakness, tenderness, or vulnerability. She made this intolerance clear enough with me every time I spoke, as if I was simply not getting it right—in short, never good enough. What was interesting and difficult about this experience was that I found myself not only carefully tread-ing on eggshells, similar to her experience with her mother, but also feeling increasingly paralysed in my capacity to think, as if my men-tal space was narrowing, without any room to manoeuvre under her watchful eye.

She would often fire one question after another, initially about my status, times of each session, or the content of my comments to her. It was clear that she had profound doubts about anything I offered her and whether it was really for her benefit, often ridiculing the whole idea of seeking help. It was not so much the content of her question-ing but her manner that got under my skin. It suggested to me that she was trying to communicate how enmeshed or invaded she felt with her own mother by giving me an experience of invading *my* personal space. This type of invasive experience is often indicative of a brittle mental structure that cannot tolerate any space that includes a third object. It is a world of black-and-white, binary thinking, (literally, in this case, with her choice of sexual partners). She demonstrated her unconscious rac-ism by telling me how well-travelled and broad-minded she was about other races and cultures different to hers, so much so that she felt very comfortable about dating Black men, all told in a patronising way. The unspoken belief was that they (and I) were vulnerable Black men who needed her patronage.

She was keen to tell me, quite triumphantly that, in contrast, her par-ents were typically middle-class and narrow-minded and how worried she was about her parents' reaction to her Black boyfriend. They men-tioned a story in the newspapers of a Black teenager being murdered by White youths in a local neighbourhood, which she heard as an instance of her parent's intolerance and attempt to sabotage her relationship by frightening her about the dangers of her boyfriend. I thought the patient was now struggling with her own narrow-mindedness and intolerance, which she managed to project into her parents. This had to do with her own unconscious fears and hostility of relating to a Black person (relating to anybody, for that matter), defensively covered up by her apparent open-mindedness. Her manner of relating to me and the fear and contempt she had for anything "psychological" suggested that fears about her own unconscious mind were concretely equated with black skin, which constituted a phobic object.

At some level, she was aware that she had a strong capacity to destroy anything good and therefore life-enhancing. This was a concern that brought her to treatment and now this transferred to me, with her anxiety that our working together would suffer a similar fate.

Internally, this concern about whether her good feelings or destructiveness would prevail could be understood in terms of the attitudes she witnessed from her parents. A mother who was disturbed and cruel to others, with a father who tried to passively accept this type of assault and pretend it was of little significance. The patient identified with both the cruelty of her mother and a different type of madness from her father, who had turned a blind eye to something awful happening in the family. Given this inner state of affairs, her dominant anxiety was about her capacity to abort any fruitful outcome of an intercourse between herself and her partners, a mixed-race baby or, symbolically, a therapeutic baby in the form of understanding and being understood.

In moment to moment interactions with me, she would try to abort anything I said to her even though there were fleeting moments when a warmer and more tender part of her would appreciate feeling understood. Moments of curiosity about me, when she would ponder about my ethnicity, which country I had come from, whether or not I had a family, and so on, would be followed by a backlash. The experience of reflection and concern would then be followed by abrupt plans for an extended break that would disrupt her treatment.

It felt as if she had aborted any fruitful work we had done together, and the next session would feel like starting-over again. In the interim she would have psychically re-assembled all her defensive manoeuvres that had been momentarily challenged by me, and then attack me with a vengeance, devaluing my help by requesting to see another therapist. Moments of feeling dependent or vulnerable with me felt to her like a narcissistic blow, a wound that she nursed with revenge as she tried to regain control of me. Despite her complaint that her father never stood firm against her mother's onslaughts, she resented my standing-firm to her when she became identified with her mother's cruel behaviour.

When there was some faint hope that a strong, benign figure could contain her destructiveness it was immediately attacked.

Overview

Her choice of Black sexual partners is interesting because it has a number of meanings and functions for this patient. I want to focus on a specific theme that has to do with her treatment of her own feelings of fragility or vulnerability. Her partners were African research students working in a university with her, who were relatively new to the country and somewhat dependent on her. One might say that they acquiesced to her control much like she experienced her father.

Was black skin a psychic bolt-hole; an escape into a concretely different skin as a way of fleeing from an internal object that was felt to be intolerable? Perhaps the escape into black skin was a concrete attempt to punctuate a contrast from her mother's skin and presence, a wedge to fend off anxieties to do with profound fears of feeling invaded by her disturbance. The internal separation, one imagines, would have been all the more difficult to do in the face of a relatively weak or impotent father who seemed unable to help her in this task.

This hypothesis would view her repetition of forming and attacking her intimate relationships as a function of her flight from an intolerable and intolerant object with whom she needed to become dependent, but then felt increasingly trapped with these feelings. Perhaps her intense ambivalence fuelled an oscillating pattern that she felt could only be controlled by splitting. Black African partners were unconsciously chosen to facilitate an internal split whereby her infantile feelings could be projected into them. However, the trouble started when this splitting no longer served its function—that is to say when she started to become more dependent on them. When her objects stepped out of line in this way, her charitable feelings towards her Black partners merged into the background as her own intolerance surfaced and gave expression to racist thinking in her narcissistic superiority and contempt for them. She was the White Florence Nightingale rescuing the vulnerable and dependent Black child/partner/therapist, enabling her not only to distance herself from these feelings but treat them in a sadistic manner, perhaps as she experienced her own mother doing.

Her psychic equilibrium was disturbed every time her needs started to surface in relation to me or her partners, which was when she would drop them ruthlessly, get into a state of guilt-ridden panic and despair, and move on to the next relationship. She had fleeting moments of understanding this destructive pattern that brought her into treatment where the internal problem was now being repeated in relation to me, this time with an Asian man.

The underlying dynamics in her repetitive behaviour would have followed the same course with any clinician, regardless of their ethnicity, but in this situation our salient differences became an opportune pathway for an internal situation to become more readily available for the splitting and projection of unwanted feelings. There is little doubt that the immediacy and intensity with which these processes operated tell us something about the relative and varying strengths of liveliness and deadness of the internal situation. The main casualties were obviously herself and her Black partners, who could do no right, while in the transference my experience of treading delicately with her reflected the pressures she was exerting to re-enact a sadomasochistic relationship. This she could cruelly exploit by trying to make me into a devalued object, needing her, repeating her experience as a child of treading carefully with a disturbing and disturbed mother.

Just as her father expected her to "shut up and put up" with her mother's disturbance her partners were not there to question her actions, and I was not to disturb her psychic equilibrium. I was to know my place in the consulting room, and keep quiet while she treated me in any way she chose. This was the internal template that opportunistically utilised our ethnic differences to facilitate the racist thinking that was keeping her psychic equilibrium in place.

She attempted this by not allowing me to even slightly step outside my assigned position. This meant my interpretations or changes in session times and breaks imposed by me had to be carefully monitored. These interventions put her in touch with her needs, which was intolerable for her. In her mind I had stepped out of line by exercising a capacity for thinking, coupling with my own thoughts and actions that did not include her. In this way she could externalise and communicate to me a brutal inner world that she herself was caught up in, one that did not allow herself any independence.

Not being allowed to step out of my "assigned position" reflects the fear of thinking, which is then projected into the therapist who feels he has to tread cautiously. Her attempt to ridicule or reject whatever I put to her was an attempt to establish a cruel and hateful contact with me by trying to make me feel small. However, it reflected the type of contact she had in relation to an aspect of herself, the infantile and vulnerable part of her personality that she hated and despised. She was accustomed to projecting this part of herself into others, namely her boyfriends and now me. This type of cruelty did not emerge as long as her dependency was untouched, but the tables turned once this defensive organisation was threatened in the treatment situation.

Moments of silence between us, in which I was thinking about what she was saying, would often feel intolerable to her and she would be overcome with paranoid anxieties of what was going through my mind. This prompted her to fire questions at me in an attempt to get us away from an internal persecutory state which, without being more fully understood, could not be tolerated.

In contrast were silences that she initiated herself, where she could keep me guessing or invite me to pursue her and thereby experience me as hounding her, as further evidence to support her inability to trust and engage with me. However, in keeping me waiting she was also letting me know that it was I who needed help, not her. If I stepped out of line, by using my mind and keeping to my task, I would be met with further comments that were aimed at trying to make me feel inadequate or small and insignificant, indicative of how she felt inside in relation to her own sense of vulnerability.

On brief occasions when she felt understood by me, this would be followed by a renewed attempt to attack my help and understanding. The experience of feeling understood was itself persecutory because it made her feel more fragile, needy, and dependent on me. Her telling me that she feared falling into pieces if she let go of her control would suggest an identification with her mother's fragile state, with no experience of a container for an uncontained mind.

What is interesting is the possible unconscious connection between the experience of her mother's "black" moods and the Black men who were symbolically like, but unlike, her mother's state of mind. When she equated the two, her intimacy with her partners felt like she was getting too close to an insane object in the form of her mother—a contact that she feared would fragment her mind into pieces. Internally, this closeness to her mother was experienced as catastrophic, as she feared something explosive and violent took place with intimate contact, which she then had to escape from by becoming self-sufficient. Hence the claustro-agoraphobic dilemma (Rey, 1979) in this patient's inner life, which she was re-enacting with her Black partners and repeating with me.

CHAPTER FOUR

The racist gaze: bearing witness

This chapter explores the psychological consequences of being at the receiving end of racism. It is a malignancy that has many faces, both overt and covert. To be told relentlessly that you are inferior or not good enough is to experience a daily assault on the self that involves not only what is unwittingly said in words and gestures but what is not said. Unconscious racism in everyday living impinges silently on the psyche, affecting feelings of self-worth. The formulation I have been developing in this book regards the thwarting of others' potency as a key dynamic in racism. It raises important issues about the impact of this type of assault on the capacity for freedom of thought and flexibility in the mind of the individual, as well as the therapeutic challenges of engaging with this phenomenon when it emerges in the consulting room.

Patient E: naming the unnameable

A Black Nigerian man came to see me for his anxiety following a car accident. When he arrived at my consulting room he looked cautious as he spoke to me about the accident. I was particularly struck by the tone of his voice, which was somewhat hesitant, as if he was treading carefully with me. He said a car suddenly accelerated in his workplace car park and hit his own car while he was waiting for a space. The patient came out of the car shocked and annoyed asking the other driver for his insurance details, but he said the driver refused to do this which left him feeling angry and frustrated. His anger turned to outrage when the White staff at the reception desk wanted to see his insurance details and other bits of paperwork but would not reciprocate his request in relation to the other driver.

He said the staff were behaving as if he was at fault. He had a feeling something was going on. He hesitated for a while and looked at me saying: "I am not being funny but something was going on here … I try not to think like this but it's happened to me before … I know something was going on here …" He repeated this several times, which made me think that he was trying to make a plea that something awful had been happening to him, which both he and I needed convincing about. He felt he would not be believed. He went on to tell me that the driver who crashed into him was a White man who worked as a senior official in the same organisation as himself.

There are different levels on which this communication can be understood in relation to who was not hearing him properly, but for the present purpose I want to focus on the way this patient's immediate predicament is shaped by his experience of the White world at large, in which people going about their ordinary lives can experience a moment of madness in which racist thinking and feeling confronts them or ambushes their ordinary sensibilities. This man felt something awful was happening to him when he was asked for his papers, which he felt had to do with him being Black, but he could not be sure, despite a feeling that he was being misused in a way that could not be made sense of or articulated in any other way. He tries to explain it away to make his life less conflicted and painful but he feels that doing so would also be a betrayal of a truth that is demanding recognition. I believe his plea had to do with wanting me to both witness and assist him in naming an experience that was unnameable.

I would have liked to have nudged him towards a recognition that was beginning to take shape in his mind, but I think I may have become a little impatient and named what he may have been feeling perhaps because I found his agony difficult to bear. I said to him that he was trying to tell me that he felt he was being misused because he was Black.

He looked visibly relieved and somewhat surprised at what he heard. I put it to him that he seemed a little taken aback that this type of painful experience could be thought about with me. He said he would not be able to say this to everybody, but who was really going to believe an angry Black man? He said he tried so hard not to fall into the typical stereotype of an angry Black man but he could not get it right because the way he was being treated made him feel angry.

Listening to this patient's account brought the image of Kafka's trial (1925) to my mind, as if Black people often find themselves trapped in a Kafkaesque world from which there is no escape. Any reasonable plea for fairness made in his defence is used as evidence against him by the "prosecution", because to argue his case at all is to unleash the spectre of the aggressive Black man trying to intimidate you and "get away with it". He starts from the position of assumed guilt, and from there it is an uphill, if not an impossible struggle to establish his innocence. Because it is left for him alone to disentangle his convoluted and agonising experience, this desperate scenario is what first needs recognition before further understanding can follow. This was perhaps what I picked up on in his plea for empathy, which required a willingness to name the painful experience before he could mobilise his capacity to think freely again.

After this moment of recognition, he gave himself the space to think about other episodes that also pained and baffled him, describing an incident at his son's nursery when a White member of staff had taken his son's soiled pants and put them into a bag with his clean clothes, so that all the clothes were covered in faeces. The patient was furious that something so thoughtless had occurred, especially as it was a member of staff whom he had a suspicion was not taking kindly to his boisterous son. He said he had a feeling that his son was being ill-treated.

The staff member's ordinary capacity to think was ambushed by equating the little boy's black skin with his faeces, resulting in all his clothes being smeared. Otherwise it would have been a normal occurrence in a nursery for the clothes to be placed in separate bags. Was this a racist moment in the staff-member that turned the patient's child into faeces to be got rid of? My patient felt something was very wrong here, but it was something which he could not fully recognise nor articulate. In the car park he was not only trying to manage the emotional impact of a physical trauma from the collision but another type of assault that involved his mistreatment at the reception desk. At the nursery, he was confronted with a faecal assault on his son's identity which also affected his capacity to think. This may explain why he needed a third person to first witness his predicament in order to pave the way towards more joined-up thinking that could help him articulate and make sense of his experience. I suggest that a space where triangulation can occur in the therapist's mind is a starting point for the traumatised patient to repair the fractures in his own thinking that becomes temporarily damaged in racism.

Vignette I: the furniture delivery man

When I was living in South Africa, a conversation with a furniture delivery man made me think further about the attacks on thinking that take place on those at the receiving end of racism. This man rang me to say he had my address but did not know how to find me geographically. I asked him whether he was as new to this place as I was, to which the reply came he knew where I was on the map but the area I was living in was historically a White area, and he never ventured into that part of town. This was despite the fact that we were now in the new South Africa, twelve years after the end of official apartheid. He was inviting me to understand that he was faced with an internal situation that neither he nor I fully understood at the time. I directed him to where I was staying, but also found myself feeling slightly perplexed at the significance of what he had just told me and enquiring about this with him. This conversation has stayed with me.

I thought it was not the external world he wanted help in navigating but the internal geography of his mind, an area that perhaps mirrored a split that was state-imposed in a country that had partitioned-off races and social spaces so that venturing across the divide would have been potentially calamitous. I wondered what had become paralysed inside his mind that made it so difficult to think, in a man who otherwise seemed quite capable of doing his job. What did he want me to do for him, psychically, that he seemed unable to do for himself? As this man was not a patient of mine, my hypothesis about his inner functioning has to remain tentative but may help in building up a picture of what might take place in a racist assault.

I wondered if his phobic reaction reflected an inner situation that was pocketed away or partitioned-off in his mind, creating an internal apartheid that was effectively sealed-off from conscious awareness or access. Perhaps this had become an encapsulated space within which the traumatic experience and the associated pain and defences are repeatedly re-enacted (Hopper, 1991). It is possible that this may have become triggered when he had to exercise a new freedom of movement that he was not accustomed to, such as travelling to a so-called White area. In this internal apartheid, which functioned like a state-sanctioned gang in his mind, he felt unable to think about and separate out past from present, despite being intellectually aware of the fact that official apartheid no longer existed.

On reflection, the furniture delivery man had unconsciously invited me to bear witness to a phenomenon of a racist past living in the present by bringing me the furniture of his mind that had become temporarily scrambled when faced with a new challenge. The "White area" acted like a phobic object. My guidance required an inquiry about how things had come to be this way for him, which I had not purposefully set out to do when I began giving him directions to my address. It was clear that he was temporarily unable to think about navigating this particular task because the problem lay elsewhere in the deeper recesses of his mind. His capacity to think was either weak, damaged, or temporarily unavailable to him when he was faced with the task of re-integrating an area of his mind that had become frozen in time, like a psychic time-capsule that was oblivious to the changing realities. However, it held his emotional life to ransom because it was an area outside the process of thinking and metabolising the painful feelings associated with his experience of apartheid. Our brief conversation on the phone may have been the catalyst for an experience of a third object that could begin to mediate a space that was hitherto too difficult to think about.

When he arrived to my address it was clear that he was overcome with much feeling of having found my place. He stared out of the window of the apartment for a few minutes and said: "You know, there was a time when people like you and I would not have been able to walk out there." This comment, and the implicit feeling of both relief and sadness, conveyed to me that he was experiencing an important moment of separating out in his mind what once took place in history but was no longer the case. It was another time and place. I thought it was the beginning of a process inside him that had yet to be made sense of in the fullness of time.

This observation resonates with what Bollas (2015) refers to as the "return of the oppressed":

> The oppressed refers to the suspension or distortion of human thinking. The repressed returns through the rerouting of ideas. The oppressed refers to an alteration not of the *contents* of the mind, but of the *capacities* of the mind—the way one forms thoughts. When discussing the course of oppression, we note a cumulative degradation of the *forms* of perception, thought and communication. (p. 539, author's italics)
>
> The oppressed *is* to be found in the unconscious but as a *failed effort*, the trace of what might have been ideationally created (even if banished) and linking up to other forms of such failure. The cumulative effect of thousands of such failed possibilities forms a network of *the mangled*—of ideas half formed but left disabled. The history of this sad evolution leaves the self at a loss, in a state of unconscious grief, and a mourning that, if it goes unrecognised, can be endless. (pp. 539–540)

While the two men in these vignettes did not pose particular difficulties or challenges in reaching them emotionally, the situation is markedly different when trying to think with a person who needs to enact his or her inner disturbance in a more volatile way. Here, only two possibilities exist in the patient's mind—victim or perpetrator—which pose particular types of challenges in thinking and understanding the patient in a humane way. This is difficult for both patient and therapist as the murderousness of racism that emerges in the consulting room can not only sabotage the healthy, functioning aspects of the individual but also attack the therapist's mind and work.

Patient F

A Black African man's early life was characterised by physical and verbal racist assaults at the hands of his Black father who became floridly psychotic from time to time, believing that he could wash his son's black skin colour to make him White.

This was witnessed by his mother, who felt unable to intervene directly as she was also a victim of his violence. Attempts to mitigate a family tragedy were met with another twist of fate when his mother sent him to a boarding school to protect him from his father, where he suffered further racism. Not only was his psychological integrity attacked by the racist assault from his father, but his mother's relative passivity in the face of these assaults represented another type of failure of containment. It also compelled him to bear witness to his mother's experience as an impotent observer.

This laid the foundations for identifications with different states of mind—being a victim of assault, a witness vicariously terrorised but too impotent to act, and a third identification with a racist object. Fortunately for him there was a more positive intervention, albeit a mixed blessing, when he was sent to the boarding school, which at least prevented a potential homicide by his father. The patient triumphed over his own terror of helplessness by getting others to feel vulnerable and terrorised when he was involved in a world of criminality. He was an observer as well as a participant, one might say an impotent observer, being swept along by fast-moving events that often landed him in prison. There were elements of high drama in situations involving the police that echoed some of the experiences in his early years, when the police had to be called when his father was out of control. For the patient, however, the police were seen as both enemy and ally, a crucial third object whom he wished to involve as a potent and potentially sane figure of authority that could intervene when he started to become volatile like his father. Perhaps this is why he told me he was often relieved when he was placed in prison. However, once there, his fate often took a turn for the worse as he experienced further brutality inside prison, mirroring his early experiences of being beaten by his father and being bullied at boarding school.

Some of the dynamics of his experience were often enacted with me in the consulting room when, under the grip of a racist object, based on his father, his murderous thinking took hold in his wish to peel off his black skin. He said he wanted to make his pain more tolerable by removing his black skin from the gaze of White people, which he felt had brought him nothing but trouble, both in his early life and later from racist projections in the world outside. He sought refuge in what he considered to be a safe place, the desire to have white skin, which took on suicidal overtones when it echoed his father's murderous attitude during his psychotic episodes.

These situations would be enacted with me in various ways that indicated a troubled relationship to his sense of self, expressed concretely through the racist meanings he attached to his skin colour. He tested whether he could trust me to help him by becoming provocative about my own colour, searching for ways to gauge how I felt about my brown skin. He often looked me up and down and perceived my suit as indicative of having "sold out" to the White establishment. His doubts about my capacity to help him concealed his own feelings of anger and guilt about what he had done to his good feelings about being Black. By projecting the negative feelings and the guilt, he could look at me accusingly as the one who had "sold out" and betrayed his Black-self. This was sometimes done through a "tit-for-tat" strategy in reverse, by trying to devalue my help on the grounds of my not being black enough, with his wish to have a "proper" Black therapist.

In this way, he would try to give me the experience of what it felt like to feel inferior and rejected, reanimating the ghost of his racist father who tried to beat all the blackness out of him. I felt that some of his provocative behaviours were attempts to take me back to that place of terror in his childhood.

On one occasion he was furious about what he felt were the subtle gestures of White people who looked nervous in his proximity. There was little doubt that this was also a reference to his perception of me, a situation that created a curious split in how this was experienced in and out of the consulting room. Some of my colleagues outside the consulting room felt more alarmed than I was when they heard him shouting, and were concerned whether they should intervene for my safety. On reflection, we thought that this may have been an enactment of a splitting and possibly even a dissociative process that reflected the patient's early experience of what could and could not be allowed to be emotionally acknowledged under a racist assault of his mind. This was in contrast to those on the outside, perhaps like his mother and siblings, helpless themselves and bearing witness to helplessness through the beatings taking place on the other side of the door. Because this experience could not be processed by him, the only means available to communicate his terror was through repetition, via a process whereby the "audience" and participants experienced contrasting feelings inside and outside.

When patients are compelled to do to others what has been done to them they are experiencing a moment in which only two possibilities seem to exist in their mind—victim and perpetrator. Perhaps his search for mastery, to inflict what was passively received, was in the service of being heard, seen, or witnessed. In these circumstances, the therapist would be challenged to experience an element of the psychic impotence that the patient suffered *and* be able to recover enough to exercise his potency to continue thinking with the patient, unlike his earlier experience. This reflective space involves being both a participant and an observer—an experience that traumatised patients cannot access or one that is weak and absent in their functioning.

This difficulty is linked to the capacity for symbolic thinking, which becomes the main casualty in trauma (Garland, 1998). Symbolisation acts like a bridge between the event and the person experiencing it so that overwhelming events can be thought about and processed, enabling them to be integrated into the rest of the personality rather than remain sequestered away. This is in sharp contrast to patient F's internal situation, where feelings were either evacuated or reacted to in a passive way. A third possibility lay in the potential to create a symbolic space to think and process rather than remaining a passive witness or observer. This possibility also paved the way for fostering the patient's growing curiosity about himself, which was expressed through his attempts to provoke me. For example, he could become patronising by lecturing me about Black history, trying to convince me that he was proud of being Black, which I felt also concealed his own anxieties about his precarious identity. Yet I felt he was a young man trying to search and look for a good father to help him explore his own identity in a safe way by "poking and prodding" at my Asian identity, not unlike a parent watching their child discover and assert their own sense of personal agency. His annoying cockiness was designed to evoke a response from me in relation to his potency that had been tragically crushed by his father but was now surfacing again in varied and various ways.

I thought that he needed the safety of a space to flex his muscles and experiment with his aggression in ways that were different to his brutal experience with racism. This involved searching for and discovering good aspects of his Black-self that were buried, but given fresh life through his curiosity about me. He started to discover different aspects of his cultural history and good Black role models to identify with. The therapeutic challenge was to enable a more benign couple to exist in his inner world, where different aspects of himself, Black and White, could co-exist rather than be drawn into the murderousness of a racist solution to his difficulties.

From the conflicts he was struggling with in his psychic life it was important for him to test how comfortable I was in my own skin, in all its symbolic meanings—whether I would easily shatter or retaliate and render his sense of trust and safety at risk, or whether I was permeable but robust enough to continue thinking with him. Most crucially, would I continue to value him as a person worthy of help in the face of his attacks on me? This is particularly poignant for a man whose experience was not only of being chronically devalued by the racism of his father, and many of his experiences in the world at large, but also the experience of some of his earliest relations with his mother, despite what seemed to be her good intentions.[1]

For this patient, the racist object within had ambushed his whole personality. Early psychic disasters (of which I have focused only on one: his relationship to his racist father) created profound failures in containment that became repeated in a most painful and dramatic way. This involved the use of skin and skin colour as a stage on which to enact painful conflicts to do with his struggle to acquire a more authentic sense of himself. When he used his black skin as a target for his aggression, as his father had done to him, he was left with all the self-hatred staring him in the face, which he wanted to eliminate by peeling off his skin. However, the graver problem was how his skin surface and colour had become not only the stage on which to enact his grievances and desire for revenge on the people who had failed him, but also the site of his most powerful identification. Any attempt to seek revenge on them using the medium of his skin then became a suicidal gesture.

Survivors of racist hatred, violence, and, indeed, trauma in general have experienced either a psychic assault on their mind through sheer force, or something more silent and insidious which often renders them helpless and unable to think about the experience. This violent rupture in the continuity of self and experience inevitably affects the person's basic trust and sense of safety, throwing profound doubt on the reliability of both their internal and external objects. The problem of linkage to other potentially fragile areas of the mind that the racist assault can trigger would also give these doubts particular poignancy.

One of the therapeutic challenges is to be able to create a space for ourselves as therapists, allowing a freedom of movement in thinking and feeling under the watchful eyes of our patients, who need to observe, emotionally "poke and prod" us, and experience our struggle to reach them, in the hope that eventually they, in turn, are better able to exercise their own freedom of movement. This type of freedom is anathema to the racist state of mind, which is impermeable—lacking a capacity for truly creative thought, self-reflection, or empathy. Its malignancy can manifest in indifference or a wish to devalue, debase, humiliate, and shame the self and all its links to a good and fruitful inner object world whose very fabric or protective skin is attacked.

The naming of an experience that is so often caught up with feelings of weakness, shame, and humiliation often invites, overtly or covertly, another mind to bear witness, imagine, empathise, and articulate an inner struggle that cannot be voiced. This brings to the fore painful issues of what has been lost through aggression by others, and responsibility for one's collusion with the destructiveness of racism. The painstaking process of psychotherapy or analysis can enable possibilities for the traumatic event to be integrated into the rest of the self or personality. The self is then no longer defined solely by the trauma but is separated from it and more able to exercise a new kind of freedom and rhythm of movement in thinking and feeling. This involves a healthy vigilance (in contrast to the hyper-vigilance in trauma) that also gives the Black victim the courage to bear witness to, name, and protect the self from the subtle and overt ravages of the racism of everyday life, rather than turning a blind eye to it in a vain attempt to deny its existence.

CHAPTER FIVE

Clinical and theoretical challenges

A t the heart of our clinical work is a preoccupation with understanding the kinds of anxieties and quality of thinking in
particular states of mind that obstruct the desire to learn and
acquire knowledge about ourselves in relation to others in the world.
This creates challenges in the consulting room for patient and therapist
when preoccupations about racial or cultural differences emerge in the
patient's mind. This includes racist perceptions that need close and sensitive scrutiny to capture the nuances of what is being grappled with
and communicated.

It raises the question as to what extent psychoanalytic theory and
technique can engage with the subtleties of these preoccupations when
even speaking to the experience of racism is difficult enough outside the
consulting room with colleagues, let alone working with the myriad of
emotional forces at play between therapist and patient. In this respect,
institutions are as vulnerable as individuals, each facing the challenge
of creating a space to think when the subject matter is inherently antag-
onistic to such a project.

Some of the pitfalls in the structure of racist thinking can become
re-enacted in our theorising, conversations, and professional discussions, leading to an impression of furthering our knowledge but closing

off any prospect of a depth to understanding. In short, there is a risk of our thinking and language being stripped of a sense of curiosity, depth, and meaning, repeating the dynamics of how the ethnic other is treated in racism. Our conversations and texts can be left high and dry, where something vital is sanitised (Ward, 1988). This raises an important issue as to what we hope to achieve clinically when analysing race and racism in the consulting room.

As far as the consulting room is concerned, working with unconscious fantasies involving ethnicity, culture, race, or racism can and should be our business to address thoughtfully. The central question is always to do with the functions of these states of mind at any given moment and the degree to which they obstruct the capacity to relate to oneself and others in a humane way. This requires following the patient's imagination closely, the subtle trajectories of which can move to and fro, between racist hostility at one end of the spectrum, towards curiosity, concern, and learning at the other extreme. The first trajectory is destructive and anti-developmental in nature; the second is more hopeful, borne out of an acknowledgement of loss and mourning in accommodating the ethnic other.

We are unlikely to ever get patients coming into therapy or analysis requesting help with their propensity for racist thinking and feeling, but like all defensive strategies, they require our attention and sensitivity in how we approach them. Any therapeutic engagement with a racist state of mind will involve a careful assessment of the degree to which a benign presence or object relationship can be mobilised in the individual that could act as a counterweight to the malignant presence in the personality, whether this is a temporary phenomenon or a permanent fixture. These deep structures of thought and feeling, as ultimate defences against the loss of identity, can surface in any encounter between patient and therapist, but perhaps, most poignantly, when both have salient differences in terms of their racial or cultural backgrounds. It also raises the interesting question of what happens to the subject matter of race or racism and its intra-psychic content when patient and therapist are from apparently similar backgrounds.

The material that emerges can provide a potential avenue for exploring the self, yet the psychoanalytic profession has been relatively slow to investigate the subtleties of this topic in the consulting room. This picture has been gradually changing, with a growing momentum in recent years that is bearing fruit (e.g., Davids, 2011; Holmes, 1992;

Kareem & Littlewood, 1992; Leary, 1995; Lousada, 2006; Moodley & Palmer, 2006; Tan, 1994; Timimi, 1996). The relative absence of close scrutiny or, worse, the negation of this subject matter from the consulting room, is something I take up in the next section of the book, arguing that this omission may reflect enactments that keep oppressive social arrangements in place in ways that mirror structural racism in society.

Psychoanalysis and the psychotherapies have often perceived issues to do with ethnicity or race, quite defensively, as external issues of less significance than the preoccupations with the inner world of the patient and the transference relationship, rather than seeing these attributes as integral to psychic life and the therapeutic process. It is not an exaggeration to say that this attitude risks repeating, through a lack of engagement within the consulting room, the dynamics of splitting, marginalising, and cleansing characteristics of racist thinking. Just as we are all vulnerable to repeat our private narratives, so too can our theoretical frameworks suffer the same fate through their repetition on the plane of ethnicity. They are as vulnerable as the people who create them.

Conceptual blind spots

Concepts of race, culture, and ethnicity are not fixed entities but ideas and ideologies that are dynamic and in constant flux, changing in relation to the prevailing social, economic, cultural, and political practices (Dalal, 2006; Ferber, 1998). Ideologies are also predicated on notions of power and privilege, which they try to justify or legitimise by giving authority to particular ways of being. They often involve notions of the right and correct way to think and be, or present themselves as the sole possessors of truth. Attempting to understand these ideologies requires vigilance over the potential problems of using concepts in ways that can mirror the need for absolute certainty in racism.

This is important because these concepts sometimes get thought and talked about as if they are static things one carries around in one's pocket, which can even become institutionalised as a body of knowledge and practice (Ahmad, 1996). For example, in matters to do with the idea or concept of "culture" in the consulting room it is worth thinking about what meanings are attributed to this by the patient and how they are to be understood. We do not necessarily know. The essentially hybrid nature of human identity, in which we cannot help but be transformed in subtle ways in the very process of interaction with others, raises important questions as to whether our concepts or ideas reflect this dynamism in a meaningful way.

Dalal (2006) argues that to talk about qualities of difference and similarity as absolute states, which many clinicians do, creates a false impression. He quotes the well-known example of the anxiety about strangeness and strangers in early life, thought to be re-activated in meeting strangers in adult life (e.g., Basche-Kahre, 1984). But Black and White strangers evoke differing reactions because both are embodied with different meanings in the external and internal worlds. In the opening chapter, with my example of the Black teenager in the playground, would the aversion have been of the same magnitude if the new arrival had been white or brown? It raises important issues of whether the notion of the stranger as an abstraction sufficiently addresses this complexity, yet clinicians have become accustomed to speaking about these concepts in a two-dimensional way, removed from the lived experience of being the ethnic other in a White world.

The crucial issue in therapy or analysis appears to be not the difference or similarity *per se*, but understanding the function or purpose of drawing on one or the other of these attributes at any given moment with the patient. This brings us to consider the particular use to which concepts are brought into play in our patients' communication. At one extreme, differences may be completely denied, commonly referred to as the White liberal position, which sees only the person and not the colour or ethnicity. At the other end of the spectrum, there is a heightened awareness of difference which is used specifically for the hatred of others. In contrast are preoccupations about others, driven more by a sense of curiosity about difference and similarity and a wish for intimacy and connection. The challenge is to work out, in a meaningful way, the significance of these preoccupations and dynamics in the context of all that the patient brings to us. These states of mind serve particular functions in the structure of the ego which will vary from one individual to the next.

Ethnic matching

Perhaps because of structural inequalities along racial lines manifest in the experience of racism, the idea of matching patient and therapist on grounds of perceived similarity of ethnicity was both therapeutically appealing and contentious. Matching therapists, for example, with their patients' ethnicity was thought to facilitate the positive transference or the "therapeutic alliance", a partnership in the service of understanding the patient's difficulties in the context of their experience, in this case, of racism. Here the idea of matching was based on the assumption that the experience of strangeness and alienation on the part of the patient was minimised, facilitating trust and empathy.

It is not too difficult to see how this argument might apply in a situation where a Black person has become traumatised from a racist attack by a White person, which might culminate in the patient being thrown into a suspicious or even paranoid state of mind where concrete thinking predominates. The Black person's capacity for discriminating between the racist and White people in general, a faculty that needs symbolic thinking, may become the first casualty of the traumatic incident. He may therefore insist on being seen only by a therapist from what he perceives to be the safety of his own ethnic background, which may become concretised in skin colour or other attributes. This may only be a temporary strategy for coping, and understandable, from the point of view of his psychic state. Whether or not the actual reality meets the patient's expectations is another matter.

How these matters are dealt with depends on the varied positions that therapists and institutions adopt as part of their working practices. The decision to comply with the patient's request can be an opportunity to understand the patient's conscious and unconscious reasoning behind the concreteness of their choice. Alternatively, to comply may be thought of as an unhelpful collusion with the patient's internal difficulties. Clinically, it makes sense to consider the individual circumstances of each case. Ultimately, if there is no patient in the consulting room then there is no opportunity to find out anything about the motivation in their request.

There are issues that need to be addressed explicitly before decisions are made, such as what characteristics are being considered for matching. Is it possible to "match" a concept as diverse as ethnic or racial identity without reducing it to concrete categories like skin colour or which part of the world one comes from?

Some of the reasons for seeking to match therapist and patient on grounds of ethnicity are motivated by sensitivity and empathy about certain types of experiences that affect one ethnic group more than another, such as racism. There is mileage in the argument that some therapists' mental antennae are not tuned-in to these painful daily experiences of living for people of Black and other ethnic communities, and that as a consequence they fail to be picked up adequately and understood. This view needs to be balanced with the risks of placing emphasis only on external events and not enough on links to the inner world of the patient. I am caricaturing the argument, but it is self-evident that both extremes are a potential disservice to the patient.

The central difficulty is in sustaining the principles of triangularity—maintaining a link between the patient's experience of inner and outer reality so that complexity and indeterminacy can be tolerated and thought about, rather than reduced to a wish for certainty.

The therapist's ethnicity

Much of the impetus in thinking closely about the significance of the therapist's ethnicity came at the height of the civil rights movement in America, when turbulent relations between Blacks and Whites provided the motivation to study its impact on the dynamics that emerged in the treatment relationship.

While early research focused on the psychological effects of discriminatory laws and racial prejudice from Whites (Jones, 1974), this shifted into looking closely at the many levels of unconscious meaning which the overt differences in ethnicity between therapist and patient entailed.

Curry (1964), an early pioneer in the field, revealed how his black skin colour, the most salient marker of his difference, unconsciously evoked a variety of contradictory fantasies and images in his White patient. This included notions of being endowed with extraordinary sexuality, lack of inhibition, intellectual inferiority (Carter & Haislip, 1972), an idealised maternal object in the form of the indulgent "mammy" (Grier, 1967), or evil, darkness, doom, and despair. Faeces, dirt, and danger have also been some of the features linked to the notion of blackness (Sherwood, 1980).

Curry argued that these images had their basis in the prevalent socio-cultural beliefs, which were a complex amalgam of racial attitudes or stereotypes that he subsumed under the term "pre-transference". He argued that these pre-conceptions (Bion, 1961) became intertwined with intra-psychic conflicts to generate anxieties in the patient that led to the consequent denigration of the therapist and the therapeutic process. In the context of the American civil unrest of the 1960s, he was preoccupied by the incongruence of the natural asymmetry between therapist and patient with the racial status prevalent between Blacks and Whites at the time. Typical problems included White patients refusing to enter treatment with what they considered to be an inferior Black therapist, or the opposite, a denial of the therapist's ethnicity. Some patients over-identified with him as a member of a minority group, which often concealed hostility or contempt towards him (Griffith, 1977; Cavenar & Spaulding, 1978).

Some have commented on the envy underlying the idealisation of Black therapists as individuals who, despite obstacles, are perceived to have managed to become secure in themselves, unlike the patient. While this can provide much hope for the patient, such idealisation can mask doubts about the capability of the Black therapist. However, the veneer of pleasure and admiration of the therapist can contain within it a twist by which the patient can cling to the idea that both patient and therapist are victims of suffering. Behind this is a hidden belief that it could have been worse—the patient might have had a black skin himself, thus making the clinician the worse off. In the White patient's mind this can render his Black therapist, and the therapeutic work, potentially impotent.

Navigating the counter-transference

Counter-transference reactions offer a potential opportunity to listen in a way that enables us to understand the kinds of emotional pressures and predicaments that both patient and therapist may be put under to behave in one way or another. Until recently, there was a conspicuous absence of thinking about counter-transference reactions in relation to ethnicity and racism in the consulting room, thus blocking a potential avenue for understanding the internal world of the patient.

Thoughtful scrutiny and discussion as to why clinicians, regardless of their ethnicity, may choose to work with patients from certain ethnic communities over others tends to be avoided. Just as the motivating factors for working with any patient need to be understood, so it is the case in this area as part of the overall thinking and management of the patient. This allows a better understanding of how potential strengths or weaknesses in the therapist may play out in the therapeutic work.

While some have argued that because the experience of racism—a common feature of most Black people's lives—simply does not feature in the White experience, clinicians from this background will give it less prominence in their listening and capacity to empathise. In my view, the problem goes beyond skin colour or ethnicity. I am reminded of a conversation with a Black colleague who decided only to work with Black patients, as he felt no longer able to cope with, nor wanted to deal with, the racist projections of his White patients. In an understandable attempt to minimise his pain, he had wrongly assumed that their shared heritage would eliminate all sources of superiority/inferiority, idealisation, or contempt of him. These can remain hidden behind the wish to seek out a Black therapist as a safe space to be understood and leaves the patient ultimately vulnerable in this area of functioning.

To sidestep this part of therapeutic work is to misunderstand how racism operates. Structural racism is a powerful ideological and emotional template that puts us all under pressure, in the subtlest of ways, to behave according to unconsciously-ascribed roles specific to our ethnicities (Keval, 2013). It is part of a historical dynamic that repeats itself on the stage of society and even infiltrates the intimate space of the consulting room, where its interaction with individual character adds further complications. Since the destructive dynamic utilises the category of race or colour it becomes a problem for all of us to grapple with in one way or another.

In relation to White therapists, some of the main obstacles that have been described in the literature have to do with the unconscious guilt of the clinician working with predominantly Black patients, many of whom may have suffered the ravages of poverty, racism, and psychological deprivation. Some of the early literature focused on the unconscious guilt that was evoked in working with Black patients, which was "acted-out" in various ways, such as the tendency to sidestep the negative transference and avoid becoming the bad object for the patient. This was driven by a wish to overcompensate for the patient and appease the guilt by becoming overly polite, sympathetic, or supportive, sometimes undercharging the patient (Goldberg, Myers, & Zeifman, 1974), such as becoming lax in the collection of fees or letting sessions run over time. This type of defensiveness and "acting-out" on the part of the clinician needs to be reflected upon to understand what may be being co-enacted with his patient, providing a valuable avenue for a deeper understanding of what his patient may be struggling with.

In an attempt to keep things cosy and preserve politeness, unconscious fantasies associated with the ethnicity of the clinician are often defended against—fantasies that the patient may be too ashamed to consciously acknowledge. When both patient and therapist cannot allow themselves to think about the significance of these ideas, what is ultimately communicated is that the therapist is not resilient enough to allow such an exploration of the complex feelings that underlie both the perceived and actual differences in the room. Not only is the patient's hostility short-circuited but also the growth of their potential curiosity and healthy attachment, creating a lost opportunity to understand the patient in a meaningful way (Thomas, 1992).

The patient's envy of his clinician and his capacity to help is an inevitable part of any therapeutic work, but may prove to be a real obstacle when working with deprived patients. White therapists have been known to become rather more active and concrete in the transference, being subtly drawn in to attempts to put right the environmental wrongs that they feel are responsible for the patient's predicament rather than listen to the material closely in an attempt to understand what is behind the patient's envy. Unfortunately, these subtle enactments can sometimes feed into concrete thinking, which often forms the underlying structure of racist thinking.

In the context of Black therapists working with Black patients, one observation that has been made is the tendency of the therapist to be rather harsh in the transference when the patient is behaving as if they want to be White. It is suggested that the judgmental attitude is related in part to unresolved feelings connected to the therapist's own ethnicity. This has also been linked to the observation about Black therapists becoming too nurturing. Often, a Black patient's contempt that their therapist "sold out" to the Whites in order to be successful is sidestepped by the Black clinician. It can cover up feelings of past rejections and ridicule in the patient and bring to the surface a painful reality of failed achievements and the effect that racism and oppression may have had on curtailing opportunities for the patient. This is particularly so when the toxicity of these external experiences dovetails into some of the patient's inner difficulties. Hidden envy can perpetuate the patient's low self-image and impede his development within the consulting room and beyond.

Often, feelings of guilt and aggression are intertwined in countertransference reactions, each fostering the other in a vicious cycle. For example, unconscious prejudice in therapists who perceive themselves to be superior to their Black patients, or anxieties emanating from other racist stereotypes or perceptions about working with Black people (Thomas, 1962; Jackson, 1973) can evoke unconscious guilt. This can either be utilised as part of a self-scrutiny in the service of understanding the patient better or it can be co-opted or recruited by the patient unconsciously in enacting a destructive dynamic as part of their ongoing problem.

Patient F: shame, guilt and the negative transference

This patient, who I discussed in the previous chapter, tried to assess my capacity to help him in various ways and may have picked up on some of my anxieties about working with him, given what I knew about some of his volatile behaviour with others. At our initial meeting, he asked me various questions about my experience of working with Black people, particular those in poverty (looking me up and down, and at my suit and tie as he spoke) and then made belittling comments before asking for a Black therapist whom he felt would understand him better. While I tried to take this up in terms of his anxiety about working with me, and specifically what it was he felt I had not understood, I think he picked up my anxiety about working with him—perhaps from my tone of voice rather than anything specific I said to him. Perhaps knowing about his history and background of criminality had affected me more than I had consciously realised. As he later told me, he could use this part of his history to appear menacing and instil fear in others when he was in prison.

In the course of his therapy, I slowly realised that I had replaced close scrutiny of my anxieties of working with him with a tough front, in order to cope with his criticism and close scrutiny of me. It looked like a display of macho posturing and allowed me to conceal my anxiety of working with him as a difficult and potentially dangerous patient. But it may have been more than this. My anxiety could have had another element to it, which had to do with having got caught up with a racist perception of him that equated his blackness with criminality. His criminal record dovetailed too neatly into a racist stereotype that often sees Black people as muggers and thieves, overtly aggressive, or menacing. The reality was that he was a Black man who had been a thief and could be aggressive, menacing, and exploitative—none of which had anything exclusively or necessarily to do with his ethnicity, which a racist perception would have us believe. He was a man in deep pain whose crucial problem was his capacity to exploit others by making them frightened of him, thereby leading to him suffering rejection, incarceration, and punishment. This left him triumphant and contemptuous towards others and, ultimately, over his more weak and vulnerable self.

On reflection, I thought that his question was also asking me whether I had examined my own beliefs about him as a Black person, both positive and negative, and the motivation for working with him. Too often in this area of work one can be too eager to interpret the patient's anxiety of the clinician's resilience and not apply sufficient scrutiny to the therapist's own feelings about the patient. These are difficult to disentangle from the patient's projections, but the therapist's anxiety is often picked up through the patient's unconscious antennae—a communication that usually remains hidden in the manifest content of the clinical material.

Some of my patient's thinking suggested that he was preoccupied with a number of issues to do with both his and my safety and resilience. For example, was he sizing me up because he felt he might harm or frighten me—and would I be rendered, emotionally, too vulnerable to help him? Was I going to retaliate and harm him by intruding into his mind to put his trust and wellbeing at further risk? Would this attack come in the guise of trying to rescue him as a victim of White racism (shifting the focus from our therapeutic relationship to outside the consulting room) and leave him, potentially, internally powerless? Would this attack come by using him like a feather in my cap or, indeed, the institution's narcissistic display of how it caters for Black patients? Or would the attack come in the passive form of trying to show that I was not a racist but a liberal, tolerant, Asian therapist?

There was also a question of whether I could give myself the space to think carefully about a number of issues, such as the possibility of not working with him if I thought psychotherapeutic work was not going to be helpful or that we were not an appropriate setting to help him. What also needed to be considered was whether we were a suitable couple to work together. Needless to say, what and how this is conveyed to a patient requires much sensitivity and skill, both of which can become compromised in the heat of the moment but are of crucial importance to the wellbeing of the patient, who was desperate for help but pushing away attempts to reach him.

Many of these feelings are present in the opening gambits of a first meeting and are tested in various ways. In view of his turbulent history of attachments, the patient was quite rightly testing not only me but the institution I worked in to see whether we were up to the job we claimed we could do. This involved his assessment of whether we were comfortable and robust enough in our skin to be able to help him with his deep sense of inferiority as a Black man, which he concealed by appearing menacing to others. It is possible that his request for a Black therapist (aside from other reasons) evidenced a wish to be helped to be comfortable in his own black skin, and he could only see this happening if both he and his therapist shared the same skin colour.

Inevitably, there were moments when I failed to understand him properly; however, when we could talk more freely he would talk about his experiences, primarily of racial hatred from White people, that he was afraid would not be understood by anyone who was not Black. He firmly located this capacity in skin colour. The complaint did not strike me as unusual but the analytic task was to hear this complaint properly and to locate it in the larger picture of the patient's presentation—in other words, to listen out for who else in the patient's inner world failed to hear his true distress. My task was to continue thinking with him about this by conveying that it was possible, despite his profound doubts about me.

When the atmosphere in the room is so persecutory or paranoid, suggesting what is going on inside the mind of the patient can feel like unwanted interpretations that he is not ready to assimilate are being forced upon him. If interpretations can be like food for the mind they can also, at times, be indigestible. Sometimes, the patient perceives, quite rightly, that the intervention comes more from the therapist's anxiety than from an empathic attempt to understand. Locating the interpretation in terms of the patient's experience of the therapist can sometimes free the situation up from the oppressive atmosphere and make it more manageable, because it focuses on the patient's experience of what may be going on in the therapist's mind (Steiner, 1993). At other moments of impasse, where it has felt appropriate, I have been inclined to exercise my own curiosity aloud about the atmosphere in the room between the two of us, which puts the observation in a third place (as if it was an external object) that invites the patients' curiosity without placing too much pressure on them. Through various difficult moments like these my patient could see that he had managed to rattle but not throw me, moments in which both he and I had to "soak up" something about each other that was essentially human—that something important could be learnt about his experience through both of us being emotionally affected in the encounter.

As we gradually came to understand, he was harbouring consider-able guilt about the shoddy treatment of his Black-self by his own racist attitudes, which had complex origins. The attack on my suitability, as an Asian therapist, was partly related to his own tendency not to accept me in the same way that he was treating his vulnerable Black-self, of which he was deeply ashamed. It became clear why he wanted a Black therapist: he was searching for a therapist who could be comfortable in his own skin so as to be able to help the patient feel more comfortable in *his* own skin, and not treat it so shoddily. Ironically, this treatment involved getting rid of and projecting his blackness onto my brown skin, which he saw as not good enough. He was prone to split this part of himself off and project it onto others, irrespective of their ethnicity, so that lurking in the shadows of my brown skin, or any skin colour for that matter, was the black skin and Black-self he despised. His idealisa-tion of all things Black concealed his contempt and his wish to be White, in the hope that this would ultimately make him more lovable and give him a lifetime of immunity from further racist hatred.

It was poignantly described in his wish to peel off his black skin, a skin which he felt only brought him endless pain. He was doing to his skin what had been done to him, in a very concrete way, when he was at the receiving end of racist attacks on his Black identity as a child. Unable to process such a painful experience, he could only enact the violence on himself or towards my skin, communicating his desperation from the depths of his despair.

The attack on my skin colour, a concrete target, shifted the locus of thinking and feeling from the symbolic to the concrete. During these moments, I experienced an inability to think, as if I had been plunged temporarily into a psychotic state where my internal connections or links in thinking were dismantled. I suspect that by attempting to dismantle my potency in this way, he was communicating his own struggle to stay emotionally alive and potent in the face of his own cruelty that attacked both himself and others in this same way. His unconscious guilt arising from this type of cruelty could be easily disowned and located in others, thereby absolving him of responsibility in the matter.

Altman (2006) gives a vivid account of how feelings of hidden shame and guilt on the part of both patient and therapist can be easily recruited in the clinical situation to create a destructive enactment that needs careful scrutiny if the patient is to be helped to come to grips with it. He described some difficulties he found with a Black male patient who seemed determined to repetitively re-enact a destructive coupling that seemed to originate in his relation to his own father, and was repeated in the transference by him failing to pay his fees. Both analyst and patient were unwittingly caught up in a projective process that opportunistically used the unconscious racial stereotypes each held about the other (patient as "black criminal"/analyst as a "greedy Jew").

Altman later reflects that this scenario derived its power from his reluctance to examine his own feelings of shame and guilt arising from his racist perceptions of his patient, which made it difficult for him to understand and confront him when he was becoming destructive in treatment. Altman's relative impotence in the face of his Black patient's passive-aggressiveness was reinforced because of his own fear of being accused of becoming a White racist or a "greedy Jew". What this account suggests is that when therapists avoid scrutinising their own racial or ethnic counter-transference, they are prone to falling prey to an opportunistic process that racism feeds on, and unwittingly run the risk of re-enactment in the treatment.

Furthermore, because the enactment operates on the principle of dyadic thinking, where the dichotomous roles of "victim" and "perpetrator" are mutually played out, the only possibility of rescue is the creation of an analytic third—a space for examining how one is about to or has already got caught up in the enactment, and what this may tell us about the nature of the patient's internal and external struggles. This means tuning in to a myriad of thoughts, feelings, and fantasies about the patient, including his or her ethnicity, and racist thoughts and feelings that need careful scrutiny.

Historically, the general consensus was to explore and work through unconscious fears and fantasies in relation to ethnicity to avoid what was seen as a disruption to the analytic process (e.g., Curry, 1964). However, much like the history of the concept of counter-transference, it became apparent that reference to ethnicity in the patient's mind was often the first sign of the development of the transference relationship and could act as a catalyst for its rapid unfolding to enable the exploration of deep and meaningful issues for the patient (Schacter & Butts, 1968).

Contemporary psychoanalysis and psychotherapy would capitalise all the patients' preoccupations about his analyst/therapist, both positive and negative, conscious and unconscious, under the totality of the whole situation of the transference (Joseph, 1985). Nevertheless, working with racist projections, in all their subtlety, is no easy matter for a Black therapist, and requires a capacity to contain the patient's feelings about his race or ethnicity and acknowledge that his patient may feel terribly ashamed of having a therapist who is not White, but also how bad he is likely to feel at having such feelings of shame. What functions these feelings serve for the patient at any given moment also needs addressing in a sensitive way that enables the patient to feel safe enough to become more curious about himself. When these feelings are not addressed in the transference the risk is of the patient terminating the therapy for fear of being "found out" and exposing his vulnerability. The patient may leave in order to protect the therapist, whose reluctance to address the "racial transference" may be perceived as an area of fragility that the patient feels obliged to protect. This can leave the patient uncontained and risks him acting-out the unpalatable feelings with other people.

The challenge, therefore, is in how to understand and attend to this material in a way that is helpful for the patient. Toxic states of mind which underpin racist thinking and feeling are often so formidable and resistant to reason that they can frequently lead therapists into enactments or partial enactments of an internal situation that is heavily laden with various degrees of cruelty. If a patient manages to touch a vulnerable area in the therapist's psyche he can quite easily be recruited into becoming accusatory or judgmental of the patient's racial hostility, reflecting an internal situation in which the patient is in the grip of a sadistic superego that he feels caught up with. How to create a space in which one can remain emotionally involved and continue to think remains a challenge.

Mayes and Soth (1986) suggest that Black clinicians need to examine their feelings about their own race or ethnic identity to avoid identifying with the negative and oppressive aspects of the social system. They make the sensible argument that a strong and stable sense of unconscious and conscious security, self-worth, and self-value enables the clinician to be more mindful of moments when he is being asked to absorb or accept a denigrating or idealising projection from his patient, rather than get caught up in it and collude with the unhealthy parts of his own, and the patient's, personality.

I would argue that this applies to all therapists, who resist looking at these unpalatable feelings and their deeper significance. Perhaps

they fear accusations of being too sensitive about their colour or ethnicity, not having come to terms with it, or having some kind of chip
on their shoulder. Often there is simply an absence of a thinking space
in the supervisory relationship where these issues can be brought up
for closer scrutiny. This may reflect a wider problem within an institution that turns a blind eye to the seriousness of the situation under the
assumption that such matters are less important than the "deeper stuff"
that is thought to be where the "real" problem lies. There is no getting
around the fact that these feelings have to be lived out and known in
the "here and now" of the transference situation, whatever the ethnicity of the therapist, so that they can be processed and understood for
what they are.

We all grapple with universal conflicts to do with loving and hateful
feelings, both within ourselves and towards others, and so it is with
our patients. However, when the retreat of superiority is sought out it
is usually because these feelings are more easily rationalised than more
tender or loving feelings or the raw and primitive emotional states associated with racist hatred. Only when the patient feels his therapist can
contain these unpalatable feelings can he feel more able to contain them
within himself. The toxicity of a racist state of mind is then rendered less
influential in the patient's functioning and better managed at times of
internal or external crisis or stress, when it is usually called into action.

As Winnicott (1947) pointed out, hateful feelings are inevitable in all
of us—it is the uses to which we put these that are of ultimate concern
for our clinical work. I would add that racist thoughts and feelings are
of a different magnitude and probably produce feelings of shame and
guilt that are even more difficult to acknowledge and contend with.
There is, however, no immunity against these unpleasant emotions,
despite the seductive belief that sheer exertion of will and good nature
will serve as an antidote to the toxicity associated with racist thinking
and feeling. Instead, what is required is an attitude of vigilance rather
than trying to overcome these forces by conscious goodwill.

In the final analysis it requires tolerance for working with the narcissistic injury of recognising an aspect of our own functioning that we do
not take too kindly to and would prefer to see operating "out there", as
if it had nothing to do with us. But there is a therapeutic price for this
type of blind-spot; whether it is always possible to engage reason and
judgment in the face of such formidable forces of unreason is an interesting and challenging question.

PART III

RACE IN GROUP, ORGANISATION, AND SOCIETAL LIFE

CHAPTER SIX

Psychoanalysis and the psychotherapies: institutional cleansing

Psychoanalysis is no stranger to ethnic hatred, having been marginalised by the anti-Semitism of the Viennese, non-Jewish establishments which influenced the medical and other scientific faculties of European universities. Its unpalatable ideas about the human condition were misperceived as a reflection of Jewish temperament as a race. The holocaust that eventually unfolded in the "ethnic cleansing" and genocide of the Jews in Europe led many analysts, including Freud, to become displaced refugees. Could it be that these deeply traumatic events surface as symptoms in the way the ethnic other is treated in the body of psychoanalysis, echoing Freud's (1914) discovery that what is not remembered and worked-through is likely to be repeated?

Instead of the inner experience of the ethnic other being contained, it risks becoming marginalised and thwarted within a body of knowledge and a practice which should, one might say, know better. In this way it is given only refugee status, without a home or a receptive container that accommodates and speaks to experience across ethnicities. Having been a historical object of denigration and segregation, might this failure of understanding of the ethnic other within its own domain be a repetition of an unconscious cleansing of the subject matter?

75

One way to approach this negation is to locate it within a wider framework of understanding societal and organisational defences against anxiety (Menzies-Lyth, 1959). Psychoanalysis and the allied disciplines, the psychotherapies, can become caught up like any other field of inquiry and practice in unconscious enactments that turn a blind eye to diversity and difference in society, which get mirrored internally in its own workings. The visible portrayal of this, institutionally, is in the way various ethnic groups, particularly Black people, tend to be a relative minority if not absent as patients or as professionals in this field (Fernando, 1988). While this picture may be changing, racism's remarkable capacity to co-exist with support for ethnic and cultural diversity points to the difficulties in engaging with a psychic and social phenomenon that is cunning in nature, making it difficult to identify its workings objectively, but more noticeable if you are its victim.

Race: the institutional toilet

In a work discussion-group looking at issues of race and culture as they emerge in clinical work, I was preoccupied with the geographical positioning of our seminar room in the building. We were in the last room of the corridor at the end of the building, such that if we walked any further we would have been on our way out of the building. Perhaps this location of our space for thinking said something about where race and culture as a lived experience and subject matter was being situated unconsciously in the mind of the organisation. It was placed inside the building but on the margins, edging towards the border of being "expelled". This is significant because it mirrors some of the struggles in the subject matter, namely who or what is given significant physical and mental space between the mainstream and its margins. The relationship says something important about how a subject matter and its peoples are being treated, whether in the minds of individuals, groups, organisations, or society. It is often in these silent or subtle ways that an assault takes place in racism, which marginalises others as inadequate or inferior.

A second observation involves an organisation in which few if any of the professional therapists were from an ethnic background other than White. Members of staff from Black and other minority ethnic communities were mostly personnel who were located on the relatively junior rungs of the administrative ladder, such as reception or secretarial staff. What struck me was how common it was to see a person with a black skin colour carrying a dustpan and brush. I felt there was something compelling about this observation, since it reflected a stratification inside the organisation taking place along ethnic lines, with seniority located and associated with White staff. Black skin was associated with a junior status, and with the dustpan and brush, which raised questions about the psychic and social function of this phenomenon.

Kovel's (1970) analysis of White racism suggests that the crude, violent racism of the past that characterised the colonial mentality has become transformed into a type of violence that now operates through complex market and bureaucratic forces. The brushing aside of diverse human experiences to the margins serves both a market and a psychic economy, managing anxieties that diversity and differences stir up in the psyche and society. Powerful projective mechanisms can function to stratify and marginalise people in increasingly subtle and complex forms to keep oppressive social and economic arrangements in place. This can take place across all ethnicities, not just along the Black/White cleavage of power that racism has historically monopolised.

My image of the dustpan and brush may be telling. The unconscious denigration of black skin is reproduced socio-economically by marginalising, expelling, or cleansing-out Blacks. In this way, their inner experience is brushed into the dustbin of our ethnically stratified society, through projective mechanisms that psychically and economically lock particular ethnicities (Blacks in particular) into oppressive arrangements. These arrangements are likely to play out in ever more complex ways as our society becomes an increasingly global village with complicated migratory movements and journeys across geographical borders. According to this view, new ethnicities and cleavages of power relations will become recruited into a historical drama that institutionalises racism. This suggests that it is not only our infantile past that we are compelled to repeat but also our historical race relations at the group and societal level.

For those caught up in it, the emotional ramifications of institutionalised forms of racism are profoundly disturbing. Those on the receiving end not only fail to be properly heard and understood but feel caught up in a racist perception or gaze that does not belong to them. As I explored in an earlier chapter, this thwarts the capacity to exercise one's emotional freedom. To withhold true recognition can amount to a psychic murder, which is always present, to one degree or another, in racist attitudes that marginalise, devalue, or degrade. The subjective experience of feeling invisible or marginal is not something that has been looked at in much detail, but these conversations frequently happen behind closed doors between people of minority communities who often report a pervasive and painful feeling of being excluded or deemed invisible in a group of predominantly White people. Whether the same experience is replicated with different ethnicities is an interesting question, but it is an unconscious process that can be painfully bewildering for those on the receiving end.

Vignette II

A colleague, the only Black person amongst a White staff of clinicians, voiced her concern about the lack of space to think about Black people and their experience of racism. The response from a White colleague trying to place this on the agenda for a meeting was that some of these clinicians did not want to be thinking about all this "race stuff", they just want to get on with the work. There was an interesting silence when a question was asked as to what that meant—"to be getting on with the work".

Such a comment reflects an artificial split in which the "race stuff" is marginalised in relation to the "real" and central work of therapy. The assumption in this group was that the real work constituted depth and complexity, while issues of race are externally located and operate at the surface like skin, somewhat superficial in nature.

Here, one can see how quickly the structure of her thinking started to mirror the structure of how racism operates. First, to create an artificial split between the real and the superficial "race stuff", then projection across this divide of what is deemed to be of less value or worthy of consideration. Race is then "stuffed" (projected) with fantasies and feelings that are conveniently evacuated and disowned so that both the subject matter and the Black colleague, by implication, are unwittingly marginalised. This is an experience that Black people often consciously and unconsciously register, which leaves a feeling of being unheard or invisible.

At a small-group level, the paralysing influence of this process can sometimes be ameliorated by attempting to recognise that there is an unconscious malignant process at play even when it is difficult to name it and one cannot be sure what is going on. The recognition that there is a problem re-engages the feeling of emotional vitality that becomes temporarily attacked and paralysed by a group process which, while not overtly racist can instigate an insidious process of marginalisation on the basis of ethnic difference.

Training and supervision

Some of the understandable challenges and conundrums of engaging with this complex psychic and social problem are often met with a stance of political correctness that can unfortunately create more difficulties than it resolves. For example, current training curriculums risk mirroring racist dynamics by tagging-on issues of ethnicity, race, or racism in a rather concrete way. It is not unlike creating ethnic ghettos in society, which are apt to provide psychic pathways for racism. Attempts to speak to the subject matter sometimes end up as an area of applied work—an anthropological specimen that runs the risk of doing more to extend the conceptual boundaries of a theory than integrate the subjective experience of the ethnic other into its own theorising. This is a thorny issue that cannot be easily resolved, since it is a matter of debate when a body of theory and practice is being used to illuminate and understand the phenomenon under study or "colonise" it, repeating the very dynamics of racism in its desire to validate itself as "open" and "responsive" to these issues.

The understandable focus on the inner world of the patient within the consulting room can sometimes get caught up with a view that sees the external world as a potential source of contamination by psychosocial processes, such as racism. It is not too difficult to see that this can potentially re-create some of the very dynamics that underpin the structure of racist thought and feeling—the desire to regress to a dyadic space at the cost of a capacity to develop triangularity, which forces a recognition of the complexities of life. Perhaps as a defence against the difficulties of thinking creatively about difference and diversity one can witness attitudes of polite indifference, ignorance, and sometimes arrogance that veil anxieties to do with bewilderment, uncertainty, and fear.

Psychic life does not operate independently of the way our society has evolved along stratified lines to bolster unequal power relationships between ethnicities. In both its malignant and benign forms, racial or ethnic myths and pressures have a profound effect on one's conscious and unconscious attitudes to the developmental tasks that have to be negotiated on the path towards emotional maturity. One of the clinical challenges is to understand the inner world in the context of early life experiences and relationships situated in the ambience of the ethnic or cultural milieu, creating a mosaic of meanings to be understood in the clinical encounter.

Transference, rightly deemed the pinnacle of working analytically, also concerns the repetition of history—not only early infantile relations but ideologies that underpin the dynamics of race relations in the here and now, re-enacted from one generation to the next. One of the most challenging tasks in our professions is to understand the complexities of how infantile and ideological pasts link up in the unconscious to give shape to all that the patient brings to the consulting room.

Vignette III

A Black trainee amongst a White group of therapists in training, whom I knew to be quite vocal, gradually began to withdraw in silence in one of my teaching seminars. I thought about how I could speak to this observation without being presumptuous and intrusive. I eventually decided to speak to her directly in a separate meeting because of my concern that it might affect her learning through her lack of engagement. I simply stated my observation to her.

She said she was relieved that I had brought it up as it was something she had noticed in herself in the seminar but did not understand what was happening to her nor how she could speak about it. She had observed the same thing happening in other situations with the same group of fellow students, with whom she got on well. When I asked about her experience of the content of the seminar and discussion she was able to elaborate on how she had been feeling increasingly different and isolated as a Black person on the course, particularly when she felt much of the theoretical and clinical work did not speak to her experience as a Black woman with her own culture and customs. Instead of vocalising her views she withdrew and re-directed her anger and protest by moving her emotional experience to the margins and shutting herself off.

Aside from whatever else was going on that I was not privy to, the striking thing to witness was the change in her demeanour following our brief conversation. In subsequent seminars she was more lively and willing to debate and participate, which suggests that she had managed to recover her potency that had become temporarily paralysed in the group. This is a crucial point in the Black experience of racism, where there is an overwhelming sense of feeling powerless to speak to an experience that is difficult to name and pinpoint. There have been many anecdotal reports of this paralysing silence, which needs to be further investigated.

It is possible that a shared unconscious fantasy may be at play in these situations, ascribing dominant and submissive roles and voices according to racial/cultural categories. This shared fantasy may be taken up and used in ways that are peculiar to the individuals and groups concerned, and is not unlike how couples might function in a dysfunctional marriage or partnership (Dicks, 1967).

While, consciously, I thought the thinking in the seminar was meant to be inclusive, the Black trainee's experience suggested otherwise, culminating in a subtle shift of her experience towards the margins that was colluded with by her withdrawal.

Even my tentative attempts to speak to this seemed to have freed her up, enabling her to recover her voice. I think this phenomenon occurs in many organisations but the marginalisation is colluded with by all participants and is often difficult to name. Finding a voice representing the experience of those from non-White ethnic backgrounds in training curriculums is particularly challenging given these subtle processes of marginalisation, but my examples also provide some hope about naming and identifying them so that possibilities for change can be thought about.

Vignette IV

The clinical supervision space can be conceptualised as a triangular space, in which the supervisor's task is to assist the trainee to develop a state of mind in which he can be receptive and reflective about his work. When a supervisor reflects on the dynamics of a therapist/patient couple to make inferences about the underlying difficulties that the patient may experience, this helps the therapist create a state of mind in which he can become receptive and reflective, open to impressions and be able to take a third position, from where he can observe himself while participating with the patient. This creation of a triangular space is crucial in the therapist's development if he is to help his patient identify with and internalise a benign thinking object. However, when difficulties arise which fail to be adequately contained in supervision, these can result in the therapist feeling too vulnerable to manage the clinical situation and lead to acting-out by both therapist and patient.

The following vignette describes a situation which was reported to me in a consultation by a male Pakistani Muslim therapist who had been the subject of racist remarks with threats of overt violence in a psychotherapy group he was running. This was initially run with a female co-therapist of Spanish descent who decided to leave the institution. After the group members were told of her decision some months prior to her departure, members expressed feelings of being rejected and not good enough for the therapist to stay and work with them.

Following her departure, the group's anger and resentment turned on the Muslim therapist with a fantasy that she left because he had become violent and got rid of her. What most of these patients had in common was an early history of being adopted, the trauma of which found fertile ground in the departure of the co-therapist. Feelings of being rejected and wounded found a convenient pathway by using the Muslim therapist's ethnicity to express their hurt and wish for revenge. The predominant feeling in the group was that they had been deserted and left in the hands of a therapist who was the culprit. When two male members turned on him by making racist remarks, the therapist noted that the rest of the group watched this attack with equanimity, perhaps seeing a reversal of what they felt had been inflicted on them by the therapist couple.

While the therapist attempted to interpret some of these feelings in the group, he realised that he was faced with a gang-type mentality which was difficult to reason with. The impasse was all the more difficult to resolve as he told me he found the racist comments had temporarily affected his capacity to think coherently as if his thinking had been attacked as well. In the face of this type of assault, it was apparent that he missed his co-therapist's support and that he too had unresolved feelings about her departure. Some of these had been explored between them and jointly in supervision, but the matter of his race as a potential vehicle that could be used destructively was not discussed at all.

While the supervisor tried to help the therapist contain the destructiveness of the group, he felt that this did not address the specific issue of how his race was being used as a weapon to express their anger, nor the difficulty of managing racist projections when these are often part and parcel of daily living for people from the minority ethnic communities.

The analytic task was clear enough. One has to be receptive to the racist projections and allow oneself the wish to retaliate, but then engage the capacity to think and explore with them: what was being communicated by their wish to wound him in this way, given the departure of the co-therapist? This task would be difficult enough, given that racist projections attack the very links in thinking that one needs to be able to do, but without the support of his co-therapist and supervisor it was made more difficult still.

In this particular case the supervisor attempted to help the therapist by asking him to obtain some reading material pertaining to race issues so that he felt better contained to manage the group. This idea was meant to provide an alternative source of support for the therapist, albeit an intellectual one, in the face of the group assault, which he was now facing without the support of his co-therapist. Unfortunately, thinking about his ethnicity was lodged outside the supervision space, leaving the therapist uncontained. In the following session, one of the male patients lost control of his anger, this time threatening to hit a female patient, as if to enact an ongoing fantasy that it was the violence perpetrated by the Muslim therapist on his co-therapist that drove her to leave.

This was a group defence against acknowledging the profound feelings of rejection, loss, and rage at having suffered a "primal wound" (Verrier, 1993) from maternal abandonment, a dynamic now being repeated in the group. They found a way to communicate their experience of being dropped from the co-therapist's mind by finding a dramatic and volatile way of ensuring that they were seen and heard, getting under the therapist's skin by targeting his ethnicity to express their hurt and grievance. His ability to cope was, however, compromised, not only because of his unresolved feelings about his co-therapist's departure, but also because the supervision space did not keep the issue of his ethnicity in mind, to be explored and understood in the context of the group process. Instead, thinking about this was exported to an "adoptive mother" in the form of an idea of readings on race which was expected to contain the therapist's anxiety, mirroring a dynamic in which adopted patients are often expected to embrace their adoptive mother and new home, without having processed the complex feelings of being abandoned by their biological mothers. It leaves them with a profound feeling that a vital area of their early life has not been thought about nor articulated, but which continually haunts them in their future relationships (Samuel, 2003).

Professional practice

Professionals can face pressures both from within and outside their organisations to create certainties in their work which often prove to be untenable. This is sometimes expressed in a culture of prescriptive thinking or a "manual" for thinking that aims to short-circuit the difficulty of learning from experience and a genuine labour of ideas. Prescriptive thinking often results in a purely intellectual approach taken to the subject matter, draining it of any feeling or substance so that it becomes sanitised and safe to work with. It probably accounts for the disjunction between the experience of racism and the language used to describe it, questioning to what extent it is possible to remain engaged and able to articulate an experience that arouses many volatile feelings without explaining or sanitising it away.

The splitting of thought and feeling is a symbolic violence that is often discernible in attempts to theorise or converse about the subject in professional discussions, which sometimes make them appear two-dimensional, flat or sterile. The danger is to mimic the very simplicity and lack of depth or dimensionality that form the fabric of racist structures of thought and feeling. It can give the impression of furthering our knowledge but can close off any prospect of a depth to our understanding. In short, just as the ethnic other is treated as a one-dimensional entity in racial hatred and violence, so too is there the danger that our language and thinking will be devoid of any curiosity and imagination and suffer the same fate.

The attack on meaning can be often observed in groups engaged in discussions about race or racism, with a surprising regularity of comments about the difficulty of grasping one's thoughts and the substance of thought, as if the thoughts will slip away. Comments such as "It is difficult to articulate what I mean", "I am not making sense",

"I cannot put it into words", "It is not coming out correctly", "I am talking gibberish", "I do not know what I am saying", and so on, indicate the difficulty in creating a semantic container via the linking of words to create meaning.

Vignette V

A Black social worker was faced with a barrage of racist remarks when she visited an elderly client in her home. As her client needed to be taken into hospital for medical help, she contacted her colleagues. Upon their arrival, her White colleagues witnessed the racist abuse and refused to take the client to hospital, leaving their Black colleague to attend to the client alone. They seemed to have interpreted the "anti-racist" policy and procedures so concretely that they felt no obligation to assist their abusive client nor think about helping their Black colleague to contain the situation. Their "anti-racist" position left their Black colleague alone to deal with the vulnerable and hostile client. Had the ambulance staff and social worker been able to recover a space to think and work together collaboratively they may have been able to rescue themselves from being drawn into the client's uncontrollable anxiety and aggression.

The elderly client was already highly anxious about her feelings of helplessness and dependency and when the suggestion of being taken into hospital was made this would have elevated her anxiety even further, uncertain as she was about her safety and wellbeing. These feelings found their target in the Black social worker, who was already the object of racist hatred at the door, which became more severe when the client had to contemplate the prospect of placing her safety in her hands. Hospitals are anxiety-provoking places, but here the Black foreigner and "foreign experience" got equated concretely via skin colour. Had there been a space to disentangle and reduce her level of anxiety it would have enabled the client to receive the proper help she needed at the hospital despite her obnoxious behaviour.

On this occasion, the policing functions of statutory regulation made it difficult to think, and colluded with the very splitting that is characteristic of racist thinking and feeling. Instead of collaboration there was an attack on creating links that could have enabled more productive thinking to take place between them that would have contained both the client and the situation.

The study group: a space to explore race

Given the difficulties that can arise for both therapists and supervisors in thinking about race and racism in the clinical situation, the study-group format can bring anxieties about these issues to the surface in a less threatening manner, providing that they are thought about in a considered way. The task becomes one of enabling participants to use their own experience as a potential resource for grappling with difficult questions and issues about race. This involves creating a format for learning which relies less on prescriptive thinking and more on a free-associative approach that encourages them to observe and share their own thinking, feeling, and behaviour.

The task is to facilitate an attitude of inquiry into the way they relate to the material at hand, as a means of understanding how the phenomenon operates. This includes observing and commenting on what emerges in their relations to each other and to the consultant in the here and now of the session. In work discussions on race or racism the polarity of thinking and feeling seems to arise as a matter of course as groups grapple with a harsh superego that emerges to "police" impulses, revealing the limited space for thinking that results. Thinking becomes concrete so that words are felt like missiles, creating an accusatory atmosphere where the desire for absolute certainty barely disguises the arrogance in the claims to know what is the right and wrong way to think. These potentially paralysing moments of narrow-mindedness are usually located in certain individuals, based on their valency in the group which has unconsciously recruited them. The challenge then is how to avoid getting caught up in the grip of a judgmental superego so that a more fluid space can be created in which there is room for uncertainty and the exercise of curiosity, without the wish for foreclosure of meaning.

When the group is working well the atmosphere is palpably different because there is literally more space to breathe and think more imaginatively and fluidly, but the residue of depressive feelings is not to be underestimated. This is to be expected as the difficulties of truly engaging with the issues of ethnicity and race start to become more apparent (Keval, 2005).

CHAPTER SEVEN

Race in the life of a study group

The mad axe-man

A group of trainee mental health clinicians in their final year participated in a group-relations approach to learning (Bion, 1961). This approach invited them to use the authority of their own experience in clinical work, and the ideas raised in the lectures they attended, to explore issues that emerged in their study group. A plenary session was held at the end of each day which offered an opportunity to reflect on the experience of the whole day and for the members from several study groups to share their thinking with each other. This provided an experience of both small and large group functioning and a further source of discussion in the small study groups.

Since all the members were in the final stages of their postgraduate training, they were preoccupied with integrating different models of working and consolidating their professional identity. This is a long and arduous process where one often witnesses a frantic search for the right model, betraying a wish that it could explain everything without the experience of frustration, tension, and conflicts. These are inevitable feelings that have to be managed and worked-through to arrive at a more personally integrated way of working professionally.

The trainees regressed into re-living an adolescent process of struggling to negotiate their dependencies on their "parent" trainings while striving for independence of mind through exposure to new ideas along the way. Amidst this developmental turbulence was a new learning experience—an experiential one that posed a different kind of threat, with its focus on unconscious experience as a source of acquiring knowledge and competence.

The relative dependency on the clinic's teachers and facilitators that the new learning entailed stirred up various highly-charged fears and fantasies that became attached to the event and its staff. As I will go on to describe, some of these primitive anxieties became racialised and directed towards me as a symbol of potential threats to their identity. The unconscious imagery that emerged suggests that the group retreated into a racist, potentially violent state of mind as a means of dealing with the disturbance to their psychic equilibrium caused by the new and different learning experience. However, the development of a sense of curiosity, guilt, and concern in the mental life of the group mitigated the violence of the racism that had surfaced, temporarily changing the direction of their learning experience. I will focus on key moments that emerged in the unconscious life of the group over the duration of the week-long event.

At the beginning of the week the atmosphere in the group was tense when themes from the lectures would trigger particular types of anxieties. For example, a lecture on assessment issues with patients, regardless of their ethnicity, stirred up comments about issues to do with confidentiality and anxieties about whether the participants were being assessed by the clinic in an underhand way. This "paranoid" anxiety was concretely expressed by one member closing the window on entering the room, suggesting a wish to protect themselves from potential intrusions. One image that emerged was of "Chinese torture", while another which surfaced in the large group of the plenary session was of a mad axe-man running around the clinic in which the event was taking place. One member described it as trying hard to hang on to his previous training (and integrity) in the face of this new experience.

As the week progressed, other anxieties surfaced after a lecture on Oedipal themes, which the group experienced as a kind of psychological torture inflicted by a cruel parent or parental couple. This was followed by concrete acting-out in which two chairs were removed from the group, with a sense of anarchic triumph over the perceived cruelty of the imagined couple. It is as if the lecture had stirred up feelings of helplessness and anxieties about learning, expressed in this instance as an attack on the imaginary couple on whom they were dependent. Once I returned the chairs the following session there was some relief and a mocking defiance, which emerged in a dream that was reported by one of the participants.

In this dream a female student described that she was wearing a green uniform at a boarding school and found herself hiding behind some bushes with her peers. She saw the school's head-boy running across the grass, jumping on a log on a lake and managing to float on it without being toppled. There was a mixture of idealisation with a tone of mockery and derision. She described that her preoccupation was how to turn the brown log into a raft which they could use to escape. The anarchic mood in the group, and the dream of the head-boy jumping on the log, both had a quality of ridicule as if they were laughing at me behind the bushes, like adolescents secretly contemptuous of their parents. Painful feelings associated with learning from their experience in the present were now being circumvented through theft and escape. This defensive manoeuvre was mitigated by an acknowledgement that, despite their attacks on my competency, I had managed to avoid being toppled by them and therefore continued to make myself available to them, safeguarding resources that they could use to learn about themselves.

When I made a comment which touched on these issues, one response was that I was being a prat, and should have seen it coming, while others responded with material about their adolescent clients provoking their authority as professional carers in their own work settings. Some members could see the parallels with what was happening in the group and thought that the violent tearing-away of the chairs was one way they felt they could feel powerful when the learning was making them feel so stupid.

The next morning, they attended a lecture given by a Black therapist on the significance of race in the clinical setting before they attended the afternoon study group and found that the room in which they normally met had been taken and used for another meeting in the clinic. The study group had been moved to the adolescent department. Their initial reaction was to rebel through silence and apathy. When I linked this atmosphere to their feelings about being moved to a different setting, one member remarked that it was a humiliating experience being shifted around the clinic. Two members expressed their anger about the disruption and wanted to walk out in protest. I noted their protest lacked any mention of the morning lecture. Just as they ignored mentioning the lecture they attended on race, they were now ignoring me for not securing their room and supporting them properly.

When I commented on this omission, one member responded that he was not sure whether race was the issue and that it seemed more to do with the lecturer's own agenda; this was then followed by an intellectual discussion on other differences, such as ageism and sexism, that they also found interesting. I noted their reluctance to talk about and debate this in relation to the specific content of the lecture by diluting it into a consideration of other "-isms". The response was that it was not something that applied to them since they saw very few Black clients in their clinical work, but there was an acknowledgement that they could be insensitive to fellow Black professionals by not taking the time and trouble to pronounce their names properly. One comment was that the English could not be bothered to pronounce foreign names.

Their following remarks articulated their anger towards me—namely that I was a qualified therapist who had the power to make interpretations which they felt they had to take, followed by a comment by the female member (who had moved the chairs) that she was very "pissed off" that I had put the chairs back into the group, as if I was playing a game with them, keeping them controlled. She thought I was a nuisance, like acne that kept popping up and bothering them.

Their production of the image of the acne needed exploring. I thought their anger was to do with my thinking "Black head" that was trying to create a containing structure for them to learn about themselves, now seen as a nuisance controlling them. One comment dismissed this as rubbish while others suggested that an acne was indeed a horrible growth which if burst could be red and bloody, the colour of rage and danger, all of which was said in an excited and slightly menacing tone.

I commented that their behaviour suggested that my attempt to create a safe boundary by returning the chairs was experienced not as a benign act but as a cruel one, aimed at increasing their dependency and vulnerability so that I could control and humiliate them. I asked them to think that, in the light of this feeling in the group, just how did they perceive their own authority and function as professionals when they provided containment for their patients? A semi-thoughtful response emerged about many experiences during the week which had been thought-provoking for their own work, but time was short to process it all. Another member commented that she had never experienced anything like this before and wished she could continue her learning.

The next morning a chair was moved out of the group before I entered the room and one member mentioned her concern about the group's wish to create mayhem earlier in the week, as enacted with the chairs once again. I reminded them of the image of the mad axe-man that had been mentioned in the plenary session earlier in the week and alluded to intermittently throughout the course, asking them about where this madness resided. This freed the group up into telling me that they were furious towards me but did not know why. One member said she felt she wanted to physically beat me up.

I suggested that they had been accustomed during the week to locate difficult feelings about this new learning experience in the chairs, which represented the clinic and I as a couple, but they were now more prepared to reflect and be concerned about this way of managing their feelings. On the verge of tears, one member commented that one of the lectures she attended made her think that the image of the acne that came up in the group was really a way of attacking me and my race. I thought they had a wish to burst open this Asian man's black head and make him bleed.

I commented that their anger and rage towards me included their caricatures of me as the head-boy and the axe-man out to get them. A flurry of cynical comments followed, to the effect that all sorts of links could be made in this way and they did not mean anything. I asked them to think what made them behave like an axe-man themselves, "chopping up" the thoughtful links that were now being made in the group. The session ended with a reply that it was too dangerous to touch this subject, with group members looking at the floor rather embarrassed. In the last two sessions the mood of the group shifted significantly to more curious comments about their relative silence and reluctance to discuss the lecture on race, and how it was all getting more interesting but sad that it was coming to an end. They started to reflect on the week's experience of how they had tried, in one way or another, to prod and play games with me to test whether I was resilient enough. One member wondered what it would be like to meet and talk to me outside the group. Another commented that she had been provocative with me but found me solid, which had been reassuring for her so that now she found the prospect of leaving difficult.

An image was described of a wound that was badly stitched-up, which enabled us to look at their feeling of being emotionally injured by the learning event, from which they were beginning to recover, and using it to think and become more curious about themselves and their work. It was clear that time had run out before they were ready to leave, with a sense of betrayal about being badly "stitched-up", in the sense that they were invited to open their minds and then dropped prematurely with the ending of the group.

Overview

It is clear from this account of the study group that there are various interlocking themes. These have to do with the consolidation of professional and personal identity in the context of adolescent processes and Oedipal issues, which were enacted in relation to my authority. Each member was working this out through the unconscious life of a group engaged in a new and emotionally challenging experience that evoked primitive feelings. These became linked to my racial difference, which was first violently repudiated as a psychical representative of new knowledge, followed by a development that suggested a more creative and imaginative use of me and indicated a growing capacity for curiosity and thinking.

In terms of the dream they brought, the brown log/therapist could be used to make a raft to protect them in choppy waters, allowing them to contain and engage with learning about themselves rather than simply escape the scene. This led to further possibilities for reflection, a sense of guilt and concern for me, and a concomitant respect for what the new learning had to offer.

The images that emerged in the course of the week are, of course, very telling, starting with Chinese torture, already informing us of how quickly a new experience can become racialised in an opportunistic way when the conditions are right, so to speak, with an effortless projection into a salient concrete difference such as skin colour. From the point of view of their "paranoid" state of mind, the group perceived me as inflicting mental pain through torture, where I was experienced as a mad axe-man who was bringing to their minds new experiences of learning that felt intrusive and castrating. In this scenario, the new learning was felt to be invasive, like a concrete axe which attacked, forced, penetrated, and mutilated their existing mental equilibrium and identity to the point that they feared for their sanity. It might seem surprising that such psychological upheaval can be caused by learning something new for one's job, until one remembers the depths of emotion that learning can access, taking place as it does in the context of our most basic relationships (Salsberger-Wittenberg, Osborne, & Williams, 1993). It has been argued that the most humiliating thing one can say to a child, more damaging even than comments about their physical appearance, is that they are "stupid" (Sandler & Sandler, 1986). The desire to learn, how we learn, and what we learn are fundamental parts of our identity.

The image of the acne emerged later in the life of the group, suggesting that there had first been psychic growth in the group—a growth of understanding from the inside out. Nobody wants acne, not least an adolescent whose vanity is precarious at the best of times, but its unwelcome development often does signal the arrival of bodily and psychic changes in the maturing individual. Within the context of the group process, however, the physicality of the acne was felt to be repugnant, to be got rid of. This "black head" was a concrete symbol of my thinking with them, leading to an unwanted and ugly growth erupting from the inside out, that was experienced as a contamination, violation, and intrusion into their minds. In my view, the image of the acne was an unconscious symbol, but not a symbol in the true sense of the word, more a symbolic equation (Segal, 1957) that concretely equated the anxiety and repulsion of psychic growth with my ethnicity (the "black head"). Two objects of denigration came together in one symbol to attack what I represented.

Their hatred of the "black head" became a racist symbol but contained within it the hatred of learning anything new and different. While fear and suspicion were two ingredients, the dream suggests other key features that had a crucial bearing on whether they would escape from or engage with new learning experiences. Learning necessitates a dependent relationship which often evokes painful, primitive feelings of helplessness, frustration, hatred, and envy towards the object of dependency, feelings that originate in the original power asymmetry of the mother-infant relationship. It is not by accident then that the image of the head-boy emerges in the dream of the boarding school. Preoccupied and envious of my potency (green uniform?), their challenge was how they could use me more constructively (brown log/faeces/penis/mind) to build a secure raft (identity) using other logs (their contribution). The alternative was a wish to topple my authority and pervert their course of learning, implied in their wish to steal my potency and competence in a wholesale way rather than learn and critically evaluate what was more or less useful to them.

Envious attacks took place through the caricature of my role as a head-boy, suggesting that the mad axe-man in their fantasy tried to castrate and cut me down to size. This appears to have been motivated by a perceived threat to their own potency, which would have included their existing skills and experience. A familiar theme in racism is where feelings of inadequacy are turned into triumph over others by making them feel small or insignificant, which is also a strong feature of narcissistic pathology. The tone of mockery and ridicule, as well as the feelings of shame and embarrassment that eventually developed in the group, was consistent with this. I would suggest that the mad axe-man was a powerful symbol of how their envy attacked and spoiled possibilities for meaningful links that were being made in the group, and the learning event as a whole. Their fear of madness was their own capacity to mutilate meaning.

Symbolic violence, however, became concrete in the acting-out with the chairs and then took a more menacing turn when the "gang" mentality took over and members of the group expressed fear and pleasure in the wish to get rid of my "black head" by beating me up. I should say this was not a group in which I had a foreboding sense that I was being hated because of my being Asian, but the unfolding group process suggests that behind the veneer of civility is another realm of experience that can take over.

A racist state of mind can take grip when powerful primitive feelings are stirred up in relation to a new and foreign experience. In the presence of the physicality of difference such as skin colour, which one associates with ethnicity, the unconscious can link the two in a concrete way so that the hatred of new learning and knowledge gets placed or misplaced onto the plane of ethnicity and the primitive feelings are given a heightened intensity and noxious quality. In this frame of mind the "as if" quality present in a transferential use of the object breaks down or is so precarious that the inner sense of urgency finds an outlet and object to attack to get rid of the intolerable feeling state. In other words, the experience is felt at a level of the skin—a tangible sensory experience—like acne that has to be eradicated. In this realm of experience, the boundaries between self and other have collapsed; the other has felt to have got literally inside one's skin and has to be expunged.

This was expressed in the wish and urge to beat me up in the group or, more accurately, attack my thinking "black head" which was a nuisance to them. What stopped them, amongst other things, was their increased capacity to contain and think about their feelings in the group. Similarly, in the dream with its comical nature, the delinquent wishes of the group were counterbalanced by an attempt to work out how best to use me as an object. Towards the end of the group's life, this culminated in a growing capacity to think, a willingness to take some ownership of their projections, an increased use of symbols and metaphors, and a more critical approach to what was useful about their learning. This, in tandem with an increased sense of curiosity, responsibility, and a capacity for concern, changed the outcome of their learning experience.

CHAPTER EIGHT

Consulting to an organisation: race, food, sex, and aggression

Observations of group life can often provide fertile ground for looking at how unconscious racism emerges and what role it might play at any given moment in the life of an organisation. When I have been approached by an organisation requesting help with difficulties that they experience in relation to ethnicity, race, or racism, what usually materialises are highly complex issues to do with the perception and management of differences in the workplace. My main focus of inquiry is to do with understanding the culture of an organisation and the extent to which this is reflected in the staff group and their attitudes towards their primary tasks.

Assessing the organisation

Assessing an organisation is an ongoing activity that continues until the work is completed. It is like having a good working rudder and compass on a boat to navigate the journey of inquiry. I approach an institutional consultation with a view to exploring anxieties in relation to a task or set of tasks, to discover what mechanisms it uses to manage anxiety, what contributes to their breakdown, and how it can manage anxieties more productively.

The request for help from an organisation comes in many forms, not unlike a symptom that a patient might present to us which both reveals and conceals their underlying difficulties. In this context, requests can be for such things as "equal opportunities" or "race-awareness" training, some unspecified or vague description about difficulties related to "race and culture" in a staff or patient group, and so on. Often, requests are made for someone to teach about race or racism on a clinical course for professionals. The task of the consultant is to acknowledge and clarify the conscious request so that a deeper inquiry into what is being unconsciously requested can proceed.

A number of questions come to mind with such an inquiry: what is being asked for and what function it is likely to serve for the organisation; whether the requested solution would resolve the underlying anxieties that led to the request; and whether there might be a possibility and willingness in the organisation to understand the request differently, in a way that is better informed than what has been overtly requested. Usually, a crisis has arisen internally or in the form of external pressures. It is helpful to know where the organisation sees the request coming from, how they perceive it, and why now. Sometimes, it is a Black staff-member that has taken on the role of inviting and organising the external consultation. I would want to know why that member was chosen and allowed themselves to be chosen in this task to get some idea about what role that member may be playing in the context of the organisation. This may tell us something about where the motivation for change may be located.

In the example I have given, it may be that the responsibility for thinking about ethnicity and race has been concretely enacted by projecting and locating it in the Black member of staff. Might this be a symptom of how the institution compartmentalises any crises that occur into certain individuals or groups as a way of managing them? I like to involve the most senior person of the group, such as the manager or director, to assess the extent to which the request is sanctioned in the management hierarchy so that the institutional work is bolted-down or anchored properly before the process of thinking gets underway and a tidal wave of emotion surges up from the depths.

More often than not, the staff group report a crisis which needs resolving and are uncertain about how to approach the problem. The initial inquiry can be explored with the manager or director and then proceed with meeting the group to continue the inquiry in the form of a group consultation, to explore, gain more clarity, and arrive at a task to be worked on. The next step is to explore how the group envisages the intervention, what format the meetings will take, their timing and frequency, and over what period they will occur. It is helpful to know whether the intervention will be an ongoing process and what structures exist in the organisation to accommodate and maintain the work, or whether the thinking will be pushed aside once the work has ended.

This is not unlike assessing ego strength in a patient to examine his capacity for tolerating periods of relative uncertainty, or experiences of frustration, tension, and conflict. One is assessing how the intervention will be used and whether the organisation is interested in learning to function differently than it has become accustomed to. Various internal and external pressures in organisations make it difficult to create spaces for reflection (particularly around such "anxiogenic" issues as race or ethnicity), such that it habitually ignores the escalation of problems until a major crisis erupts. Requests for assistance in this area of work reveals deeper crises in the functioning of the organisation, with race becoming a convenient vehicle into which to locate the anxiety.

I am reminded of a staff team who felt very disappointed with me because I could not provide them with literature on racism—the subject matter they were concerned about in the context of their work. It revealed a culture of dependency that was prevalent in the group, leaving others to grapple with anxieties about ethnic differences in their staff and patient group, but not themselves. I asked what was stopping them from going to the library or bookshop to obtain such information if that was what they were really after. Concrete tasks and structures are crucial in the functioning of organisations but their psychological functions need to be carefully assessed. As well as their ostensible rationale, organisations also function in the service of satisfying (and sometimes thwarting) our most developmentally primitive needs, which become institutionalised in external realities, relatively independent of but continuing to affect the structure of psychic life (Fenichel, 1946).

The consultation process: listening to the "organisational story"

A female colleague[1] and I were invited to consult at a residential centre for people with severe and enduring mental illness where a third of the residents were Black Afro-Caribbean. The staff group had two Black counsellors and the manager was a White female. The initial request was for "some training on issues of race", which later emerged as two overt issues of concern. First, the institutional misuse of a Black counsellor, who ended up dealing with any and all difficult issues that came up in the staff's work with Black patients. Second, a concern about the level of overt racism amongst the White residents against the Blacks. The main crisis appeared to be precipitated by two factors: the decision of the Black residents to form a group of their own and a policy to introduce Afro-Caribbean cuisine into their canteen; both decisions being institutionally sanctioned.

When we set up an initial meeting with the staff group, we were given the secretary's office, a very small room, to meet in. Once again, the physical space allocated for the consultation was quite telling. The small space into which we were all expected to cram alluded to the institution's difficulty in allotting sufficient mental space to consider the topic at hand. The cramming of personal space also suggested a potential difficulty in establishing or maintaining appropriate boundaries, comically evident in the way members were bumping into each other in the meeting room. Other meanings would emerge in time. We can get a glimpse or a cross-section of a problem area and the culture of an institution by looking at how members of the institution come together in the form of a group, and how they relate to each other, their core task, and to us.

When invited to think about what they were struggling with, a few staff members asked whether we had any information to give them. The problem was yet to be defined by the group but the expectation was that we knew what this was and had a solution to it without any effort on their part or ours. One member braved it and said that the Black patients had separated themselves off and founded a support group of their own. This was perceived as a threat to both the White patients and staff, an anxiety that worsened around the time when a decision was made to introduce Afro-Caribbean cuisine into the canteen menu, which was perceived as favouritism. There was discontent from the perception that Afro-Caribbean cuisine was given preference, coupled with anxieties that the Blacks were dominating the Whites.

One association was that Black patients were getting louder, taking up too much of the staff's time and seen increasingly as a problem. In sharp contrast was the behaviour of the Black staff-member in our group who had remained silent, until he voiced how difficult it was to say anything, as a Black man, about the situation. The Black secretary decided she was not going to associate herself with the Black patients on the ward, as she came from a different part of the world and had more in common with Jewish people. She was at pains to distance herself from what was increasingly seen as a "Black problem" in the institution. The question of why the need arose for the Black patients to have a separate group and how this was negotiated with management was being evaded.

What was being communicated through this separation and how was it to be understood? Their polite behaviour towards each other was inconsistent with the explosive nature of the situation that was brewing in the organisation. We later learnt, during the tea-break, that one Black counsellor was sacked for bringing drugs onto the ward and the only other Black counsellor previous to him left the institution for reasons that remained unclear. One member said thoughtfully that something was indeed going on here—was the organisation getting rid of Black people?

The staff spoke of how difficult it was to have a difference of opinion or any open conflict between them. They described the atmosphere as "walking on eggshells". The request for us to provide concrete information at the beginning of our meeting was another attempt to maintain the equilibrium of the group—to keep it from getting disturbed. Nothing controversial would leak out which might lead to an accusation of being racist. In contrast, the opposite impulse—to be apparently open or transparent in the confession that "we are all racists"—can be a deceptive strategy to avoid culpability and can often stop any further thinking. The meaning of the tight physical space for our meeting became clearer. My colleague and I were being unconsciously told that the volume of the discussion about race and all its ramifications was to be "kept down" and allocated as little space as possible, despite their warm, inviting attitude.

Our subsequent meetings took place in a much larger room, which indicated that they had taken on board some of our comments about how much space they were willing to give to this task. One member spoke out that, for the first time, she had given some thought about Black people. Her children had Black friends but she thought nothing of it. She said she disliked Indian or Chinese food but liked Italian, so did that make her a racist? Then, with absolute certainty, affirmed "I know I am not a racist, I just don't like it". One member challenged her and asked her that if she had never tried Indian or Chinese food how did she actually know whether she liked or disliked it? Another member commented that it was an insult to dismiss all Indian food, she may dislike a particular dish but how could she dismiss all of it, and how would that attitude come across to an Indian person?

This thought-provoking question was hijacked by another comment by a member that she felt increasingly resentful at having to accommodate Afro-Caribbean food on the menu, as it had been just fine before. Having said that she thought she would give it a try. One member spoke of his mother's anxiety while being driven to Yorkshire (the media had been reporting on the riots between Asian and White youths in Bradford), when she became so anxious that she shut her car window, fearing that she would be assaulted by the Asians. This member spoke openly about how he had been brought up to believe that Asian people were smelly and dirty. He described an early memory of his father throwing a plate of spaghetti Bolognese out of the window, calling it "foreign muck". Another member spoke of how difficult it was to persuade her son (who had been mugged by a Black person) that not all Black people were thieves or muggers.

Another comment followed—that "shit goes down the system". He thought Black people were flushed out of the system, akin to "kicking the dog". What was curious was the increased self-disclosure in the group, which had a rather disturbing quality to it. The comments were made in a matter-of-fact way that lacked an awareness of how they could be experienced by either the Black members of the group or us as consultants. In other words, the degree of self-disclosure was deceptive, as if words were not being used in the service of emotional engagement, which might include thoughtfulness, but to flush away anxiety.

When we enquired about the dismissal of the Black counsellor it became apparent that he was sacked for the dereliction of his professional duty by bringing drugs onto the premises. The group, however, was more preoccupied with an idealisation of him that barely disguised their patronising attitude. Various associations emerged, such as being a "real lad", full of energy, music, fitness, and vitality. The manager, however, pointed out that their admiration was veering towards a stereotype of "a ganja-smoking Rastafarian". In a meeting like this we are also preoccupied with the subtle nuances of communication and, in this instance, both my colleague and I felt there was something artificial about the way this "thoughtful" comment was made. He was then spoken about as a thoughtful, caring man, but someone rather ineffectual. It also emerged that he was, in fact, responsible for initiating the controversial support group specifically for Black people before he was dismissed for his misdemeanours.

The atmosphere of the group changed as if somebody had read an obituary. What this Black staff-member represented in this group had become evacuated but what was not being confronted was the fact that he had stepped over the boundaries and violated an institutional policy. There was a sense that to openly acknowledge this was to be deemed a racist. Sanity prevailed, however, when one member spoke out that whatever the Black counsellor was, he was in actual fact accountable for his professional misconduct.

Overview

I want to focus primarily on how the issue of race initially triggers and then becomes entangled with concrete fantasies that illuminate the struggle between life-affirming and anti-developmental trends in the organisation. This institution's core task was to care for fragile patients who were prone to habitual acting-out rather than engaging with the difficulty of thinking about their mental pain. Thus, concrete thinking, with its concomitant processes of splitting and projection, was already a dominant mode of functioning in the culture of this patient group, which was also mirrored in the staff group. This was expressed in the manifest symptom of racism in the institution which could only be fathomed through listening to the "organisational story".

When we were contacted for a consultation the institution was starting to wake up and become alive again, expressed in the overt racial conflicts that felt unmanageable. Despite the painful and frightening repercussions, we saw these conflicts as a hopeful sign of some psychic movement happening in the organisation, which needed to be harnessed and used in the service of its development. This was a problem for an organisation whose wish, when a conflict arose, was to close the windows like the old lady in the car, to create a split between the safety of the interior, with its old familiar ways of doing things, and the perception of dangerous possibilities outside. This split was exacerbated by a system of unconscious projections that assigned Black and White members to precisely-defined roles, which functioned like an institutional straitjacket. Whites in the organisation were perceived as responsible parents who had to be reasonable and calm, wishing to keep the status quo, whereas Blacks were perceived as a bunch of adolescents who could be lively, creative, and full of energy but also regress into becoming violent thugs causing loud noise, becoming unruly, and lacking boundaries.

It is possible that we, the Asian consultants, were experienced like the gangs on the street bringing potential havoc to them. The question was, who created the institutional havoc in the first place and what was the function of doing so?

Our tacit task was to restore the equilibrium that they felt had become disturbed, bring the group back to how things were perceived as comfortable, and not to disturb it further with too much thinking and feeling. This did not square with their own wish to introduce and comply with the two new developments, the new cuisine and the separate Black patients' group. It looked to us as if they had been rather naïve about the repercussions of these institutional interventions, had panicked and wanted help with the fallout.

In the group transference, my colleague and I were first experienced by the physicality of our skin colour as something very foreign and intrusive to them. In this frame of mind, the mixing of white spaghetti and brown Bolognese sauce as a couple was simply inconceivable and could not be swallowed, let alone digested. This experience of mixing is turned into faeces. The linking of White and Black or brown identity is not felt to enrich but deplete the self and is experienced as an almost lethal contamination, which is projected into racially or culturally different others and attacked. These concrete qualities are often the first to emerge in any issues to do with race, which became associated with the task of exercising a process of inquiry, curiosity, and learning instigated by "outsiders".

This group was accustomed to not thinking. As one member put it, she had never given any thought to Black people. It was a no-thought. When you are not given any thought, you remain a "no-thing", a perceived void that can easily be used to project into. Blackness represented a mental space in the organisation that could not be thought about. Instead it was replaced with concrete projections. Now we were putting the idea on the menu, everything they had naïvely introduced into their organisation needed to be carefully scrutinised. Hidden and obscured behind the symptoms of racism were other intractable issues: how they used their authority, how boundaries were drawn, and how roles and tasks were assigned. What also needed assessing was whether or not it was possible for them to function differently and more productively together, other than retreating into a racist state of mind.

A new and different idea was invited into their organisation, through us, which we anticipated would be initially experienced as being force-fed with what was perceived as obnoxious food. The introduction of Afro-Caribbean cuisine, coupled with the perception of Black patients becoming more assertive (louder and more demanding of staff-time) was tantamount to an increase in the volume of psychic noise to do with difference and change. The digestive metaphor was revealing in the way race is used unconsciously to organise ethnic others along different zones of the body anatomy and flushed out, a fantasy that can become institutionalised. In this group, the opportunistic pathways for projection were the introduction of Afro-Caribbean cuisine and the more salient presence of the separate, Black patient group. It triggered primitive fantasies of an oral cannibalistic nature, where not only new and different food, but ideas or thoughts were experienced somatically, travelling and churning away inside stomachs, invading, devouring, poisoning, and ultimately violating their insides. In this mode of functioning new experiences were not felt to be enriching but, like Black muggers, were felt to rob and deplete the individual or the group's mental equilibrium. Diversity and difference was unconsciously experienced as a toxic external agent that was indigestible, turned into excrement and evacuated.

While the separation of the grouping and the menu was institutionally sanctioned at a conscious level, new and different food, people, thoughts, and feelings stirred up primitive paranoid anxieties that played havoc with their normal sensibilities. When and if it is felt to be indigestible, as any new idea may initially be experienced, it is turned into excrement—"foreign muck" that is felt to "muck up" the mind, like the spaghetti Bolognese that had to be thrown out of the window or "flushed out", as one staff-member put it. Race and all that is projected into it then becomes the institutional toilet. The image of the spaghetti Bolognese is a powerful and particularly telling image, and one that I will return to below, because it links up with quite fundamental anxieties to do with linking, thinking, feeling, and the integration of identity as part of the primal scene.

On this occasion, the concrete projections from the staff group managed to target a man with black skin who was already vulnerable to being ejected from the institution because of his misdemeanour.

The image of the spaghetti Bolognese at the beginning of the consultation was to let us get a sense of just how threatened they felt about our presence and the anxieties it aroused about thinking, linking, relationship, and mixture. Integrating the two was felt to be a contamination that produced a violent response, and it is curious to know what else was being hated and attacked beyond the brown sauce and white pasta. Lurking in the shadows of racist hatred is a hatred directed at a multitude of differences that are not allowed to be reconciled or integrated (Chasseguet-Smirguel, 1990).

When the institutional status quo was being disturbed by the Black patients' assertion of their identity, through a separate group from the White patients, it spelled trouble—trouble from the point of view that this type of splitting would have left both Black and White patients vulnerable to mutually-destructive projections. At one level, this state of affairs would have been entirely consistent and desirable to a mind which seeks to organise its world by using race to enable the splitting. This is what we saw happening when the racism towards the Black patient group increased. However, there was more to this hatred, and it had to do with favouritism. Put simply, White patients experienced a narcissistic injury from two sources: first, the feeling of exclusion from the increased exposure and attention that Black patients got from the staff/parents, and second, the exclusion from the Black patient group itself. This narcissistic injury turned into a sense of grievance that drove a wish for revenge by trying to inflict the same kind of injury on Black patients in all sorts of ways. As one staff-member indicated, the presence of a new cuisine was felt to be a negation of any other cuisine on the menu, not an additional contribution and therefore potential enrichment of the whole menu.

Like troubled parents (in this case a single female parent/manager), the management were seeking help with the perceived unruliness of their "adolescent" children/patients, both Black and White. I am reminded of the old lady who shut the window to escape the clash between the White and Asian youths, but she actually shut the window because it was the Asian youths whom she feared. Interestingly, the one Black staff-member who behaved unprofessionally was also described in such a way as to suggest that he contained all the institutional projections of adolescent vitality, both in its sexual and aggressive forms, including the wish to rebel against authority by testing boundaries through deviant means.

The reference to a masculine presence that was ineffectual was a communication in this group about a potent masculine authority that was lacking in the life of the organisation. The only such presence was caricatured as a ganja-smoking, irresponsible Rastafarian who could be easily corrupted, leaving the White, female manager in sole charge. The ejection of the Black staff-member was therefore a powerful communication that authority could not be trusted, particularly if it came in the form of a male and, even more so, a Black male. It was also an unconscious attack on the management/parental couple that could collaborate and produce creative and helpful ideas in managing the institution. Protests about the arrival of a new, different, and "strange" cuisine created enough drama in the organisation by seeking a racist solution that was used as a defence against thinking about and grappling with organisational issues to do with the management of authority, boundaries, respective roles, and tasks.

Racist hatred in this setting simplified the organisational complexities to a simple split in which purification is desirable and possible. It was expressed in the wish to get rid of the new Afro-Caribbean cuisine to avoid change, growth, and development through linking, mixing, or integration of different elements and ideas that might clash or conflict with each other. This organisation's many and varied underlying problems had nothing to do with skin colour or food but conveniently shifted its primary preoccupation to these, both to unconsciously reveal and conceal the true nature of its difficulties.

CHAPTER NINE

Reason and racism

A famous etching by Goya—part of an eighty-piece suite, *The Caprices*—is entitled: "El sueno de la razon produce monstrous": *The sleep of reason brings forth monsters*. It is thought to be a self-portrait, in which Goya imagines himself asleep amidst his drawing tools surrounded by demonic-looking, bat-like creatures and owls, associated in Spanish folk tradition with mystery and evil (Hughes, 2003). The etchings are thought to narrate the artist and print-maker's dark vision of humanity and the follies of mankind, based on his critique of contemporary Spanish society.

A modern-day interpretation of the etchings might depict one of our society's biggest challenges: the forces of reason in a struggle to overcome the monsters of prejudice, racism, fundamentalist ideologies, and terrorism. Yet, this picture of the power of rationality to overcome the forces of unreason has been problematic, giving the impression that reason is an innocent bystander—like Goya's innocent slumberer pounced upon by the (dark) monsters of the imagination. We could also conceive it as an unconscious collusion between the two, echoing the comments by one of my patients mentioned earlier that he was a "willing accomplice" to the havoc he created in his life.

As Cohen (2006) points out:

> In fact, it is not the sleep of reason which has produced "monstrous races"; rather it is the creatures of the racist imagination which have periodically aroused the European intelligentsia from its slumbers, if only in order to rationalize them as the basis of new technologies of surveillance and control over subject populations. (p. 246)

The powers of rationality espoused in the vision of the European Enlightenment was itself rooted in "race thinking" (Altman, 2006), equating science and rationality with maturity and civilisation. It laid the foundation for a number of dichotomies that divided those cultures deemed to be technologically, culturally, and morally advanced from those perceived to be undeveloped or "degenerate" in all these respects. This dichotomy dovetailed into a split between the rational and the primitive mind (both childlike and irrational), which provided moral justification for the colonial project of civilising "primitive" cultures by offering them enlightenment in the form of science, technology, and rationality. The Enlightenment saw clarity, explanation, and the light of reason as the ideal of self-knowledge, while all things dark, including dark-skinned peoples, constituted the realm of unreason, the unconscious, and the primitive world.

It is a gross oversimplification, but this psychic split between the rational and irrational mind provided much of the ideological fodder on which the structure of racist thought and feeling thrived throughout the colonial period and beyond. Blackness was equated with the wild, primitive, and unruly forces of the unconscious mind, which had to be tamed, expressed through the machinery of slavery and oppression, in contrast to the notions of emotional control and moral integrity associated with Whiteness (Fanon, 1952). In this way, the slave was equated with what we might now think of as the "repressed unconscious" across many cultures. For example, in the context of Black Brazilian culture, Black oppression is thought to mirror the profound repression of human instinctuality (Da Conceicao & De Lyra Chebabi, 1987) and all the characteristics one would associate with the primary process of mental functioning (Freud, 1911b).

In the Indian caste system, those with the darkest skin have been the subject of economic, psychological, and spiritual oppression, yet some of the deities of worship, such as the revered Krishna, are of dark complexion, revealing the way that elements of the repressed are allowed to emerge without conscious acknowledgement. What is interesting is that these dark deities are also credited with an extraordinary potency in both mind and body, imbued as they are with desire, fascination, and fear. Even before the advent of colonialism, there were deeply entrenched beliefs about the superiority of pale over dark skin in the context of the Aryan invasion in 1500 BC by the lighter-skinned nomads, who proceeded to inculcate their own values in succeeding generations. There is even an ancient Hindu Sanskrit belief that light skin takes away all sin (Chatterjee, 1981).

As various writers have commented, this binary thinking, in which everything is "black and white", has been used historically to perpetuate a process of domination and control through ideologies that justified power, privilege, and superiority over others (Moodley, 2006; Sashidaran, 1986). While, strictly speaking, the caste system is more hierarchical than binary, it is nevertheless based on what one might describe as "shadism"—denigration increasing as one moves further away from whiteness towards black skin. Racism exploits this in the name of reason in a cunning way, like a magician's sleight of hand, to heighten one's sense of moral superiority over others.

Exposure and consequences of societal racism

The struggle to manage a corrupt or unhealthy alliance between reason and racism is also evident in my clinical examples, where various types of defences were brought into play once the patient's racism had been exposed, which threatened their psychic integrity. Denial and manic omnipotence were quickly mobilised to avoid painful feelings of embarrassment, shame, guilt, and condemnation. However, what can be often overlooked, following a personal or institutional crisis where racism has been unleashed, is that the person, group, or organisation is often in a state of shock, feeling betrayed by a failure in their capacity for reason. Their internal state of persecution is then magnified by the external public outrage, which often follows in the wake of racist behaviour that has been made public. One might say there is both an external and internal riot, for which further defences have to be brought into play to manage the pain. Patient B, who was fleeing from a mother she accused of being racist (and restricting her freedom to be different and separate), unconsciously colluded with her and in the session with me first denied her own role in this, laughing it off as a joke, before she was able to grapple with her responsibility in the matter. She then felt better able to question and stand up to this aspect of her own functioning despite considerable anxieties about doing this. Patient C (in the care of her Black maid) harboured a racist fantasy of her inferior Black maid/therapist—remaining emotionally starved—which thwarted her life in order to justify a grievance about her early deprivation. When her racist feelings were exposed it threatened this inner arrangement that put her in an initial state of shock, followed by feelings of concern for me, before what may have been a more cunning attempt to re-instate her sense of superiority in the face of the narcissistic injury she sustained from this exposure.

The direst situation is where it is virtually impossible to think about and grapple with the guilt without taking flight, creating more racist behaviour to triumph over the pain in a perpetual repetition, not unlike patient D, who witnessed her mother's mood swings and cruelty. She took flight from engaging with her feelings of vulnerability or need, which she located in myself or her partners, who were then "aborted", risking further repetition of the pattern.

Whether reparative attempts are an expression of genuine concern is difficult to ascertain without close scrutiny. The experience of a racist thought or feeling can feel like a narcissistic injury, as one has to notice and grapple with an aspect of one's own functioning that is unpredictable and distasteful. Perhaps it is not surprising that the pain involved in such a recognition does not lend itself easily to interest or curiosity about how this state of affairs may have come about. The normal response is to condemn and expel the thought or feeling as something that does not belong to the self, group, or organisation and declare an absolute certainty in this matter.

The wish for absolute certainty is more for the purpose of re-establishing an inner equilibrium. It often takes the shape of a triumph by taking the moral high-ground rather than grappling with the complex reality of the injury, both within and outside in the public domain. The sadism of the "sinners" accused of racism then becomes evident in the "saints" who morally condemn them, leading to what Sinason (1989) has aptly described as a "dictatorship of the oppressed". It is difficult to see how any real learning can take place under this persecutory atmosphere, which only increases the likelihood that further racist situations will arise.

While the consulting room offers us an opportunity to look closely at the ways in which reason and racism can collude and create unhealthy and corrupt alliances that obstruct empathy or concern, this is more difficult to do when it comes to the cut and thrust of living with every-day racism or, indeed, incidents that have come into the public eye. Despite the speed and complexity in the way these events unfold, some of the reported narratives do, however, provide access to the underlying racist fantasies that might have been at play to obstruct proper reasoning and judgment. A case in point is of Rodney King, a Black man who was beaten senseless and senselessly by a group of police officers trying to arrest him and which sparked the Los Angeles riots in 1992 when a jury acquitted the officers. One of the police officers who arrived at the scene of the arrest had been to a previous call, to an incident of domestic disturbance, involving African-Americans, which he described as "right out of gorillas in the mist". Words such as "tunnelled in", "big time use of force", "frenzy", and boastful comments on the police in-car computer—"I haven't beaten anyone this bad in a long time"—would all suggest that a racist construction, which saw the Black man as a wild animal to be caught and beaten, eclipsed any capacity for humanity towards him. Had he not been perceived through a racist state of mind, ordinary police protocol would have been instigated to apprehend a man after a high-speed car chase. A grand jury would later hear Rodney King's testimony (as quoted in *The New York Times*, 1993): "I felt beat up and like a crushed can. That's what it felt like, like a crushed can all over, and my spirits were down real low. I can't explain it, I was in so much pain. It's hard to explain. To wake up and to tell me that I attacked some officers, I felt real bad."

Racism and football: kicking it out

An incident that received much press coverage (Prior, 2004) occurred when Ron Atkinson, a well-known football commentator made a gaff during a live radio commentary in which he muttered racist obscenities about a Black footballer, Marcel Desailly, calling him a "fucking lazy thick nigger", that, unbeknown to him, was still being broadcast live. Similar embarrassing incidents have occurred since. More recently, the sharing on social media of racist incidents at football matches has highlighted a phenomenon that was largely thought to have disappeared from the sport; accordingly, it has also received much media attention of late. How aware the commentator was of his racist thinking is unclear, or indeed whether he only realised it was racist after the public condemnation, but in the immediate aftermath of his resignation there was much speculation about the nature of his character. Many found it difficult to reconcile his temporary lapse of reason with the anti-racism work he had done in football and his support of the recruitment of Black footballers in the 1970s and 1980s—something which was deeply unpopular at the time. The emotional turmoil this created for him was evident in his subsequent attempts at reparation by trying to convince the public that he was not a racist.

Despite rallying friends and colleagues to publicly absolve him of this accusation on television, as if there could ever be a conclusive "test" to prove one's innocence in these matters, what it revealed is our society's deep unease with human contradictions when the ever-present propensity for racism breaks through conscious sensibilities in unpredictable ways.

At the very least, one could surmise that feelings of his own frustration towards the Black footballer became racialised along a well-established pathway that is all too familiar in the history of White racism towards Blacks. The racist fantasy that took hold in his mind was that this Black man had *stepped out of line* and not performed according to the White commentator's wishes. He was instead basking in pleasurable, lazy "fucking", engaged in a sexual intercourse *excluding* the commentator, when he should have been performing in line with his wishes. In this scenario, the puncture of his narcissistic control over the Black player unleashed feelings of frustration in the form of a rant, as if to relieve an inner tension that had become unbearable, which betrayed his normal capacity for reason. Yet, the racist rant, like neurotic symptoms, reveals and conceals what he may have been struggling with. It was not the footballer's "laziness" that was at issue but the commentator's wish to alleviate his disappointment and frustration through a racist perspective that could be described as "lazy thinking"—an attempt to use race as an explanation for the footballer's behaviour—when what it revealed was his own normal reasoning capacities to be corrupted by an "easy way out", and it was this that got him into deep water. He then had to contend with his feelings of shock and guilt, which he sought to alleviate through ways that created further problems for himself in the manner of a man who protests his innocence too much.

The Stephen Lawrence murder

In what was one of the biggest institutional blunders in the history of the Metropolitan Police Force in Britain, a psychological post-mortem revealed lapses that occurred in proper police procedures during an investigation into the racist murder of the Black teenager Stephen Lawrence in 1993 by a gang of White youths. A friend who was with him on the night of the racist attack, Duwayne Brooks, managed to escape, but felt that his pleas to the police who arrived at the murder scene fell on deaf ears.

Davids's (2011) analysis shows how ordinary professional functioning of the police officer who first arrived at the murder scene that evening was undermined because the two boys had been seen and experienced through a racist lens. This construction automatically directed suspicion and presumed guilt towards the Black teenagers, the police officer having also been somewhat "repulsed" by Stephen's bleeding (p. 212). The failure to pursue the assailants on the night and several failures to follow-up witness evidence, pursue leads, and make house-to-house inquiries, culminated in a bungled investigation where vital forensic evidence could not be gathered. The various blunders in the handling of the case by the police and Crown Prosecution Service, combined with the persistent demand for justice from Stephen's parents, culminated in a public inquiry which found institutionalised racism within the Metropolitan Police Force (MacPherson, 1999a). As evidence to the MacPherson inquiry from the Institute of Race Relations suggests (1999), incompetence combined with racist attitudes made for a lethal combination. I want to suggest that this incompetence amounted to failures in the capacity to think humanely, precisely because racism attacks this.

Further evidence that has come to light (Ellison, 2014) has pointed to corrupt practices that not only thwarted the inquiry but also involved the Lawrence family being monitored by the police at a time when they would have been in the throes of grief over the tragic loss of their son. This further violated their privacy, repeating the violence of intrusion that echoed the stabbing of Stephen. It is quite possible that the police suspicion and paranoia that could only see the Lawrence family in a racist gaze may have been linked indirectly to some of the extreme and vile dynamics of racism that they would have been exposed to in the course of the investigation. The targeting of the Lawrence family for close monitoring by the police force may have been caused by a, albeit less extreme, re-enactment of the original trauma via the phenomenon of secondary exposure, or so-called "vicarious trauma" (McCann & Pearlman, 1990a). I am thinking here of the video transcripts of the men accused of murdering Stephen, gathered through hidden cameras in their flat, which revealed a paranoid and sadistic fantasy world of the perpetrators, which is linked to some of the common themes I have been exploring in the narratives of racism.

Two of the main perpetrators speak of using submachine guns and knives as part of their armour to kill:

> ... every black cunt, every Paki, every copper, every mug that I know.
>
> ... I am telling you, I would take one of them, skin the black cunt alive mate, torture him, set him alight ... I would blow their two arms and legs off and say, "Go on you can swim home now". They would be bobbing around like that ...
>
> ... Look at all the niggers having a good time in the sun, all the White people getting gloomy at a bus stop ... all the niggers are having a good time at a bar drinking. A White fat bouncer ugly cunt, nice-looking Black geezer in a club having a good time and the fucking White geezer all boring—that's racist that advert ...

The segments of the video transcripts above tell us something about the discharge of sadistic impulses to mutilate Blacks once they have been dehumanised. Amongst several themes that are being narrated here, is the mutilation of the Black body, by cutting it into pieces, says something about their thinking itself—that it has been mutilated with feelings of excitement and triumph as antidotes to helplessness, impotent rage and envy in the perpetrator's minds. These feelings are enacted by thwarting Black people in their experience of pleasure or a sense of inner security and belonging in the notion of "home"—a symbolic home that the perpetrator feels robbed of and violated.

The number of occasions on which the Lawrence family were frustrated in their wish to have justice for their son, and the way in which the inquiry was thwarted so often, suggests that the violent racism that the police would have been exposed to in their investigations may have linked up unconsciously to the fertile soil of an existing, though less extreme, culture of racism in the police force. It is possible that this combination could have corrupted and ambushed some of the more rational institutional processes by attacking the possibilities of joined-up thinking that would have kept the investigation on track.

CHAPTER TEN

Thinking under fire: concluding thoughts

> ...bombing never did shorten wars (Syria) .... the Germans tried it in this country, we tried it in Dresden .... It's been tried and tried and tried and all it does is stiffen the sinews and summon up the blood.
>
> (Morpurgo, 2015)

In the face of real and imagined anxieties and fears, idealised spaces in the mind offer tempting retreats in which loyalty towards an imagined sense of community, a tribal group, or an abstraction takes precedence over the capacity for reason. Like our memories of a "happy childhood", these idealised spaces may picture a certain time, place, and customs, free of unwelcome intrusions and frustration. The past is perceived in a nostalgic haze that has become stuck in the belief that it was somehow better, more peaceful, and calmer, when there was no mixing of cultures and no need to acknowledge "other people". In contrast is the experience of diversity and difference that arouses feelings of bewilderment and uncertainty—feelings that have to be engaged, lived and worked with if the senses of loss and deprivation are to give way to accommodating the other.

This book has been preoccupied with a specific version of this state of affairs, in the form of racist states of mind. This term conveys a particular constellation of anxieties related to the feeling of being robbed or depleted, which leads to vengeful wishes to thwart and undermine the ethnic other. The quality of thinking in this state of mind also conveys something of the magnitude of the problems involved in engaging with it.

I have suggested that what underlies racist thinking is an attack on the capacities for linking, thinking, and the creation of meaning that are embodied within a productive coupling. As in the patient who could not tolerate and aborted her mixed-race baby, she could not tolerate any understanding to develop between us. This was deemed too danger-ous, because it would have created an offspring that combined the ele-ments that had to be kept separate in her psychic life. Had she allowed a mixed-race baby/insight that grew and lived, this would have repudi-ated the whole psychic arrangement of her defensive organisation.

Similarly, in a different context, "whitening" the black skin of my patient in the school playground to reassure the White kids is a powerful metaphor of how racism and other allied states of mind function, in gen-eral, to scratch out, violate, or murder differences that constitute identity. These lay out the terms on which you are deemed acceptable if you are ethnically different, and keep the dictum of "you must think and be the same as us" in place. These features share similarities with other oppres-sive states of mind, such as totalitarian thinking, fundamentalist ide-ologies, and terrorist states that function by manic omnipotence, using paranoid and projective mechanisms and processes. Such states of mind obliterate differences in thinking and feeling, allowing only those views that are officially sanctioned and enforcing them in the manner of tyran-nical, despotic, or dictatorial government regimes (McGinley, 2006).

To reason with this state of mind is deeply problematic, as one comes under relentless fire for simply thinking or attempting to think. Within the context of a tyrannical family, rather than a tyrannical state, this was demonstrated by the patient who expressed a wish to exercise an inde-pendence of mind that questioned her racist beliefs; she was met with an attitude of arrogance and threats of ostracism and violence from within herself and from members of her immediate family.

This manner of relating, like attitudes of racial superiority, invite a wish to use thuggery to break through the very defences that we are trying to reach humanely. However, when it has been possible to risk being curious and concerned, as in my experience with the study group, this salvages the seeds of hope in what might have become a bleak and hostile situation that attacked any possibilities for learning. Needless to say, these are arduous struggles towards hope when the pull towards the cruelty of racism was ever-present, as in the patient with the Black maid who expressed concern for me one moment, only to attempt to re-establish her superiority over me the next.

This kind of hopefulness is precisely what is at stake when the very institutions that we create and support in the name of reason and humanity become caught up in oppressive thinking and practices that can border on covert thuggery. I am thinking here of the British Home Office campaign in 2013 to manage illegal immigration that took the form of vans being driven around London boroughs with the slogan, "Go back home, or face arrest", while the increase in right-wing extremist groups and racism across Europe reflects the fears and fantasies echoed in Enoch Powell's speech over forty years ago. Meanwhile, the perception and treatment of vulnerable asylum seekers as "prisoners", or placing refugees in towns and cities of Britain without thinking through the extent to which it might fuel acrimony and racism in host communities, shows a reckless lack of foresight and compassion. It mirrors the apparent naivety of sanctioning an "immigration" of Afro-Caribbean cuisine into the food menu of an organisation without due consideration of how the increase in racism would have to be managed.

Demonstrations against the recent shooting of an unarmed Black man by a White police officer in Ferguson, Missouri (Swaine, 2014)—echoing the Los Angeles riots of 1992—reflects Black discontent about the underlying reality of a systemic racism that has never left American society, in which the toxic combination of colour and class determines the quality of Black people's lives. As Lane (1998) points out: "... prejudice is cogent and palpable today *because it has never left us*" (p. 3, author's italics), reflecting the phenomenon's remarkable intransigence that cautions against seeking any resolution to the problem, on the assumption that altering people's views will raise their consciousness and alter their racial prejudice. In contrast, psychoanalysis presents us with a difficult truth that Freud was preoccupied with in *Civilization and its Discontents*, which points to the assertion that human beings derive perverse pleasure from depleting the freedom of others:

> ... their neighbour is for them not only a potential helper or sexual object, but also someone who tempts them to satisfy their aggressiveness on him, to exploit his capacity for work without

compensation, to use him sexually without his consent, to seize his possessions, to humiliate him, to cause him pain, to torture and to kill him. (Freud, 1929, p. 111)

While clinical work with racism highlights the perverse pleasure gained in thwarting the ethnic other, it also tells us about other complex motives and functions of retreating into a racist state of mind, which differ from one patient to the next. Their multi-layered losses culminated in grievances and hatreds that coalesced and sought expression in a predatory, socially sanctioned, and opportunistic structure in racism which served to bind their emotional turmoil. In this way, when the shadow of the object of grievance is projected onto the ethnic other, he "presents a long awaited opportunity for the subject to enact the appalling displays of violence that heretofore have existed only internally" (Lane, 1998, p. 6).

To be at the receiving end is to experience a bewildering feeling of being caught up in an internal drama that does not belong to the stranger. He is going about his daily life, walking down the street with his shopping bags or sitting on the bus or train, and out comes a barrage of racist rants that were waiting opportunistically to attack him or, more subtly, to be picked out like my patient in the car park who was left puzzled and outraged that it was he who was interrogated for his papers, rather than his White colleague who had run into him.

All this might lead us to question whether, in the face of these formidable forces of unreason, it is possible for psychoanalysis to have any intervening and reparative power when racist fantasies are so tenacious. When there is an insistence that people must change and learn how to get along better, racist fantasies and ethnic conflicts become more volatile. This was evident when the "multicultural" food menu was officially sanctioned, but increased racial intolerance in the organisation.

The challenge of psychoanalysis is to square up to the many faces of racism, and to do so not with the aim of eliminating this type of cruelty but to interrogate the psychic investments and the complex alliances that exist between the forces of reason and racism; put another way, to understand that there are reasons for the sleep of reason.

My analysis suggests that the potentially lethal consequences of racism lie in the way anxiety and abhorrence of psychic growth and development become concretely equated with ethnicity, when two objects of denigration, as it were, come together in one symbolic and catastrophic equation. Here, "other people" are unconsciously experienced as a product of a sexual intercourse that cannot be tolerated, where my "black head", for instance, became an ugly acne to be bled and cut out; or, as in the racist retort, "you dirty fucking Paki", we have the faecal smears of a couple engaged in passionate and pleasurable "dirty" sex to create an offspring that will contaminate and invade an imagined utopia that is an irresistible retreat in the racist imagination.

I have shown that such fantasies extend to the experience of thinking itself. It demonstrates the difficulty of engaging symbolically with the impulse to expunge what is felt to be a visceral experience of the ethnic other who can be effortlessly "flushed out"—like "foreign muck", as one of the participants described in my organisational consultation.

To be a witness to the effects of racism is to acknowledge, in the words of Martin Luther King (1968) that "a riot is the language of the unheard". Those who have suffered racism have often stopped rioting in their soul and need a potent witness to engage with the wish to express outrage, recognising it as a necessary defiance that can not only be deadened by overt racism but further silenced by institutional racism. Yet, this is precisely what those on the receiving end of racism need to reclaim to re-vitalise their souls. Like the furniture delivery man who needed me to witness, puzzle over, and inquire about his state of mind so that he felt more able to begin his own process of inquiry and navigate his mind more freely; or the patient in the car park who was hesitant to name what he felt in his guts, but dare not. He was caught up internally in what many Black people experience as a Kafkaesque situation, where an expression of anger or outrage about the injustices of racism and pleas for humanity to prevail is seen as evidence of guilt, creating a straitjacket that is difficult to escape from.

Our task as clinicians is also to hear how a racist introject has managed to seep into the soul and corrode the self, while at the same time bearing witness to the outrage in a considered way. There is a distinction between courageous self-assertion and giving free rein to a murderous internal object that has corrupted legitimate outrage and turned it into emotional mayhem that can be destructive to the self and others. I am reminded of my patient whose need to assert himself and test my resilience was quite different from a wish to peel off his black skin, or assert that my own skin colour was not good enough.

I want to conclude with a vignette that captures some of the predicaments of engaging with states of mind that claim to have the sole possession of truth—an absolute knowing that can often masquerade as reason. This was an article reported in the Evening Standard on 14 January 2015, following the murder of journalists and cartoonists working in Paris for the satirical magazine *Charlie Hebdo*. A French Muslim café owner in London's Brick Lane vowed that he would not back down after receiving a death threat for displaying a sign supporting the victims of the massacre. He said a man stormed into his café demanding that he take the board down, and the following exchange took place.

> "I asked him why and he said his community was offended by it and said if I didn't remove it something bad was going to happen. I told him I was Muslim myself and I wanted to talk gently with him and I said people can't kill journalists for expressing themselves. I calmly explained to him that what he was saying was not the reality of Islam. I thought I could calm him down, but it had the opposite effect. He went crazy. He said 'I believe these people deserve to be killed and anyone supporting them deserves also to be killed'. I was all alone and started getting scared. He was a dangerous person. He said if I didn't take down the sign he would smash up the shop, and then he just left." (Dubuis, 2015)

What struck me about this conversation between the two men was the café owner's wish to remain calm in his conversation. However, what he said would have been experienced internally as anything but calming to a man already in a storm, convinced of the reality of his beliefs that the café owner was now challenging. What made the man crazy was that he had been invited to observe another possibility, "coupling up" with an alternative idea that presented a version of Islam that could tolerate difference and disagreement. Not unlike my patient who aborted any understanding that could develop between us, this man's terrorist tactics communicated an inner state that could escalate in turmoil if the café owner insisted on continuing to think with him. The owner had to stop thinking or the threat was that he, and thinking, would be killed. For the outraged "community spokesperson", the fantasy of killing was felt, at that moment, to be the only solution available that could heal the narcissistic wound from the insult to his sense of community, which had to be restored at any cost.

I was struck by how the content of this article, particularly the paranoid and violent nature of it, infected and played out in my own reflective process when thinking about including it in the book. I found myself feeling somewhat anxious that it might offend, to the extent that I or my family could be put at risk of being threatened with violence like the café owner. I thought I would leave the article out but then realised I was being terrorised by this thought and felt defiant that it was curtailing my freedom to think and observe a phenomenon that interests me. It left me with questions about whether my defiance, perhaps like the café owner and the Paris journalists, would be provocative and reckless or showed a capacity to exercise an independence of mind.

I was left undecided about the article and put the matter away until it cropped up in a discussion with a colleague, when some of this thinking was witnessed and reflected upon. It enabled me to be more at ease from the temporary grip of anxiety about thinking that I, and both participants in the café, had become caught up in. Yet it also raises difficult and challenging questions about the risks of collusion with oppressive states of mind if defiance in the name of rationality, freedom of speech, and expression is simply given as an absolute truth rather than examined for its internal complexities and contradictions.

There is no turning back the clock. Our multicultural society is becoming increasingly rich and complex, with inherent uncertainties, contradictions, pains, and pleasures that challenge our notions of an imagined community to which one can retreat. But it is a mythical structure—there is nothing to retreat to. This "menu" has to be continually grappled with, engaged with, and understood in a humane way, in contrast to the murderousness of a racist solution. There is no end-point to racism, it can be called upon at any moment using the fertile soil of our narcissistic vulnerability, but our willingness to be potent and humane witnesses, continuing to exercise the capacity to think under fire in defiance of these forces of unreason, is ultimately the ongoing container and hope for the future.

NOTES

Introduction

1. See Ward (1997) for a critique of this paradigm.

Chapter Three

1. This case study was described in Keval (2006).

Chapter Four

1. The impact of his early life is detailed in Keval (2001).

Chapter Eight

1. I am grateful to my colleague Ms. Rohina Ilyas, psychotherapist, who was my co-consultant in this work.

REFERENCES

Aron, L. (1995). The internalized primal scene. *Psychoanalytic Dialogues*, 5: 195–237.

Ahmad, W. I. U. (1996). Trouble with Culture. In: D. Kelleher & S. Hillier (Eds.), *Researching Cultural Differences in Health* (pp. 190–219). London: Routledge.

Altman, N. (2006). Black and White thinking: a psychoanalyst reconsiders race. In: R. Moodley & S. Palmer (Eds.), *Race, Culture and Psychotherapy: Critical Perspectives in Multicultural Practice* (pp. 139–149). New York: Routledge.

Anzieu, D. (1970). Skin ego. In: S. Levovici & D. Widlocher (Eds.), *Psychoanalysis in France* (pp. 17–32). New York: International Universities Press, 1980.

Basche-Kahre, E. (1984). On difficulties arising in transference and Countertransference when Analyst and Analysand have Different Socio-cultural Backgrounds. *International Review of Psychoanalysis*, 11: 61–67.

Bick, E. (1968). The experience of the skin in early object relations. *International Journal of Psycho-analysis*, 49: 484–486.

Bion, W. R. (1961). *Experiences in Groups and other papers*. London: Tavistock.

Bion, W. R. (1962a). A theory of thinking. *International Journal of Psychoanalysis*, 43: 306–310. Reprinted in E. Spillius (Ed.), *Melanie Klein Today:*

Developments in Theory and Practice, Volume 1, Mainly Theory (pp. 178–186). London: Routledge, New Library of Psychoanalysis, 1988.

Blos, P. (1962). *On Adolescence*. New York: Free Press of Glencoe.

Bollas, C. (2015). Psychoanalysis in the age of bewilderment: On the return of the oppressed. *International Journal of Psycho-analysis, 96*: 535–551.

Britton, R. (1989). The missing link: parental sexuality in the Oedipus complex. In: J. Steiner (Ed.), *The Oedipus Complex Today* (pp. 83–101). London: Karnac.

Calvo, L. (2008). Racial fantasies and the primal scene of miscegenation. *International Journal of Psycho-analysis, 89(1)*: 55–70.

Carpy, D. (1989). Tolerating the countertransference: A mutative process. *International Journal of Psychoanalysis, 70(2)*: 287–294.

Carter, J. H., & Haislip, T. M. (1972). Race and its relevance to transference. *American of Orthopsychiatry, 42*: 865–871.

Cavenar, J. O., & Spaulding, J. G. (1978). When the Psychotherapist is Black. *American Journal of Psychiatry, 135(9)*: 1084–1087.

Chassguet-Smirgel, J. (1990). Reflections of a psycho-analyst upon the Nazi biocracy and genocide. *International Review of Psycho-analysis, 17*: 167–176.

Chatterjee, M. S. (1981). Colour symbolism and the skin: some notes. *Journal of Ethnic and Migration Studies, 9(1)*: 1981.

Cohen, P. (1993). *Home Rules: Some reflections on Race and Nationalism in Everyday Life*. London: The New Ethnicities Unit, University of East London.

Cohen, P. (2006). Reason, Racism and the Popular Monster. In: B. Richards (Ed.), *Crises of the Self. Further Essays on Psychoanalysis and Politics*. London: Free Association Books.

Curry, A. E. (1964). Myth, Transference and the Black Psychotherapist. *Psychoanalytic Review, 51(D)*: 7–14.

Dalal, F. (2006). Culturalism in multicultural psychotherapy. In: R. Moodley & S. Palmer (Eds.), *Race, Culture and Psychotherapy: Critical Perspectives in Multicultural Practice* (pp. 36–45). New York: Routledge.

Davids, M. F. (2011). *Internal Racism: A Psychoanalytic Approach to Race and Difference*. Basingstoke: Palgrave Macmillan.

Da Conceicao, C. G., & De Lyra Chebabi, W. (1987). Psychoanalysis and the role of Black life and Culture in Brazil. *International Review of Psycho-analysis, 14*: 185–202.

Dicks, H. (1967). *Marital tensions, clinical studies towards a psychological theory of interaction*. London: Karnac.

Dubuis, A. (2015). Coffee shop owner faces death threats over "Je suis Charlie" sign outside Brick Lane café. Evening Standard, 14 January. Available at: www.standard.co.uk [last accessed 19 September 2015].

Ellison, M. (2014). The Stephen Lawrence Independent Review: Possible corruption and the role of undercover policing in the Stephen Lawrence case. London: HMSO (HC 1038-I). Available at: www.gov.uk/government/publications/stephen-lawrence-independent-review [last accessed 19 September 2015].

Esman, A. H. (1973). The primal scene: A review and a reconsideration. *Psychoanalytic Study of the Child*, 28: 49–82.

Fanon, F. (1967). *The Wretched of the Earth*. London: Penguin Books.

Fanon, F. (1952). *Black Skin, White Masks*. (C. L. Markmann, Trans.) London: Pluto Press, 1986.

Feldman, M. (1989). The Oedipus complex: manifestations in the inner world and the therapeutic situation In: J. Steiner (Ed.), *The Oedipus Complex Today* (pp. 103–128). London: Karnac.

Fenichel, O. (1946). *The Psychoanalytic Theory of the Neuroses*. New York: Norton.

Ferber, A. L. (1998). Constructing Whiteness: The Intersections of Race and Gender in US White Supremacist Discourse. *Ethnic and Racial Studies*, 21: 48–63.

Fernando, S. (1988). *Race and Culture in Psychiatry*. Kent: Croom Helm.

Freud, S. (1908c). On the sexual theories of children. *S.E.*, 9: 205–226. London: Hogarth.

Freud, S. (1911b). "Formulations on the Two Principles of Mental Functioning". (1911–1913): The Case of Schreber, papers on Technique and other works, *S.E.*, 12: 215–227. London: Hogarth.

Freud, S. (1914). "Remembering, Repeating and Working-Through (Further Recommendations on the Technique of Psycho-Analysis II)". (1911–1913): The Case of Schreber, Papers on Technique and Other works, *S.E.*, 12: 145–156. London: Hogarth.

Freud, S. (1917). Mourning and melancholia. *S.E.*, 14: 243–258. London: Hogarth.

Freud, S. (1918b). From the history of an infantile neurosis. *S.E.*, 17: 3–123. London: Hogarth.

Freud, S. (1930). Civilization and its discontents. *S.E.*, 21: 57–146. London: Hogarth.

Gabbard, G. O. (1993). On hate in love relationships: The narcissism of minor differences revisited. *Psychoanalytic Quarterly*, 62: 229–238.

Gadd, D. (2010). Racial hatred and unmourned loss. *Sociological Research Online*, 15(3): 1–20.

Garland, C. (Ed.) (1998). *Understanding Trauma: A Psychoanalytic Approach (Tavistock Clinic Series)*. London: Duckworth.

Gilroy, P. (2006a). *Postcolonial Melancholia*. New York: Columbia University Press.

Goldberg, E. L., Myers, W. A., & Zeifman, I. (1974). Some Observations on Three Interracial Analyses. *International Journal of Psycho-Analysis, 55*: 495–500.

Grier, W. (1967). When the therapist is negro: some effects on the treatment process. *American Journal of Psychiatry, 123*: 12.

Griffith, M. S. (1977). The influences of race on the psychotherapeutic relationship. *Psychiatry, 40(1)*: 27–40.

Hall, S. (1992). New Ethnicities. In: J. Donald & A. Rattansi (Eds.), *Race, Culture and Difference* (pp. 252–259). Buckingham: Open University Press.

Hinshelwood, R. D. (2007). Intolerance and the Intolerable: The Case of Racism. *Psychoanalysis, Culture & Society, 12*: 1–20.

Holmes, D. (1992). Race and Transference in Psychoanalysis and Psychotherapy. *International Journal of Psychoanalysis, 73*: 1–11.

Hopper, E. (1991). Encapsulation as a defence against the fear of annihilation. *International Journal of Psycho-analysis, 72*: 607–624.

Hughes, R. (2003). *Goya*. New York: Alfred. A Knopf.

Jackson, A. M. (1973). Psychotherapy factors associated with the race of the therapist. *Psychotherapy, Theory, Research & Practice, 10*: 273–277.

Jones, E. (1974). Social class and psychotherapy: A critical review of research. *Psychiatry, 37*: 307–320.

Joseph, B. (1985). Transference: The total situation. *International Journal of Psycho-analysis, 66*: 447–454.

Kafka, F. (1925). The Trial. In: *Franz Kafka* (pp. 13–128). London: Secker & Warburg/Octopus Books.

Kareem, J., & Littlewood, R. (1992). *Intercultural therapy: Themes, Interpretations and Practice*. Oxford: Blackwell Scientific Publications.

Keval, N. (2001). Understanding the trauma of racial violence in a black patient. *British Journal of Psychotherapy, 18(1)*: 34–51.

Keval, N. (2005). Racist States of Mind. In: M. Bower (Ed.), *Psychoanalytic Theory for Social Work Practice: Thinking Under Fire* (pp. 30–43). London: Routledge.

Keval, N. (2006). Understanding unbearable anxieties: the retreat into racism. In: R. Moodley & S. Palmer (Eds.) *Race, Culture and Psychotherapy, Critical Perspectives in Multicultural Practice* (pp. 150–159). New York: Routledge.

Keval, N. (2013). Racist states of mind in institutional life. *New Associations, 13*: 11.

King, Jr., M. L. (1968). *The Other America*, speech by Rev. Martin Luther King, Jr. at Grosse Pointe High School, USA, 14 March 1968. Available at: http://www.gphistorical.org/mlk/mlkspeech [last accessed 19 September 2015].

Klein, M. (1946). Notes on some schizoid mechanisms. *International Journal of Psycho-analysis, 27*: 99–110.

Kohon, G. (1986). Countertransference: An Independent view. In: G. Kohon (Ed.), *The British School Of Psychoanalysis. The Independent Tradition.* Free Association Books.

Kohon, G. (2012). The Oedipus Complex. In: P. Williams, J. Keene, & S. Dermen (Eds.), *Independent Psychoanalysis Today* (pp. 253–270). London: Karnac.

Kovel, J. (1970). *White Racism: A Psychohistory.* New York: Pantheon Press.

Lane, C. (1998). The Psychoanalysis of Race: An Introduction. In: C. Lane (Ed.), *The Psychoanalysis of Race* (pp. 1–37). New York: Columbia University Press.

Laplanche, J., & Pontalis, J. B. (1986). Fantasy and the origins of sexuality. In: V. Burgin, J. Donald, & C. Kaplan (Eds.), *Formations of Fantasy* (pp. 5–34). London: Methuen.

Larcourt, R. (16 June 1965). *ITN Reports: KKK in Britain,* ITN News. Story reference: X16066502. Available at www.itnsource.com

Leary, K. (1995). "Interpreting in the dark": Race and Ethnicity in Psychoanalytic Psychotherapy. *Psychoanalytic Psychology, 12*: 127–140.

Lousada, J. (2006). Glancing over the shoulder: Racism, fear of the stranger and the fascist state of mind. *Psychoanalytic Psychotherapy, 20(2)*: 97–104.

Mayes, S., & Soth, N. (1986). Cross-Racial Psychotherapy with the borderline patient: Should the patient fire the therapist? *Journal of Contemporary Psychotherapy, 16(2)*: 107–114.

Masotta, O. (1976). *Lecciones de Intoduccio`n al Psicoana'lisis* (Vol. 1). Barcelona: Gedisa, 1977.

McCann, I. L., & Pearlman, L. A. (1990a). Vicarious traumatization: A framework for understanding the psychological effects of working with victims. *Journal of Traumatic Stress, 3(1)*, 131–149.

McDougall, J. (1980). *Plea for a Measure of Abnormality.* New York: International Universities Press.

Macpherson, W. (1999). *The Stephen Lawrence Inquiry: Report of an Inquiry by Sir William MacPherson of Cluny.* London: HSMO (Cm 4262-I). Available at: https://www.gov.uk/government/publications/the-stephen-lawrence-inquiry [last accessed 19 September 2015].

McGinley, E. (2006). The Totalitarian State Of Mind, Editorial. *Psychoanalytic Psychotherapy, 20(2)*: 77–83.

Meltzer, D. (1973). *Sexual States of Mind.* Perthshire: Clunie.

Menzies-Lyth, I. (1959). The functioning of social systems as a defence against anxiety. *Human Relations, 13*: 95–121.

Moodley, R., & Palmer, S. (Eds). (2006). *Race, Culture and Psychotherapy. Critical Perspectives in Multicultural Practice.* London: Routledge.

Money-Kyrle, R. (1978). *The Collected Papers of Roger Money-Kyrle.* Perthshire: Clunie.

Morpurgo, M. (4th December, 2015). Michael Morpurgo interviewed by Jon Snow on Channel 4 News, 4th December 2015.

Ogden, T. H. (1989). *The Primitive Edge of Experience.* London: Karnac, 1992.

Powell, E. (1968). "Rivers of Blood", speech by Enoch Powell MP at a Conservative Association meeting in Birmingham, UK, 20 April 1968. Available at: http://www.telegraph.co.uk/comment/3643823/Enoch-Powells-Rivers-of-Blood-speech.html [last accessed 19 September 2015].

Prior, I. (22nd, April 2004). The Guardian. TV pundit Ron Atkinson sacked for his racist remark. Available at www.theguardian.com

Reicher, S., & Hopkins, N. (2001). *Self and Nation.* London: Sage Publications.

Rey, J. H. (1979). Schizoid phenomena in the borderline. In: J. LeBoit & A. Capponi (Eds). *Advances in the Psychotherapy of the Borderline Patient* (pp. 449–484). London: Jason Aronson.

Rosenfeld, H. (1971). A Clinical approach to the psychoanalytic theory of the life and death instincts: an investigation into the aggressive aspects of narcissism. *International Journal of Psychoanalysis, 52:* 169–178.

Said, E. W. (2003). *Freud and the Non-European.* London: Verso, in Association with the Freud Museum.

Samuel, H. (2003). Adoption: Some clinical features of adults who have been adopted and the difficulties of helping them in NHS Psychotherapy. *Psychoanalytic Psychotherapy, 17(3):* 206–218.

Salberger-Wittenberg, I., Osborne, E., & Williams, G. (1993). *The Emotional Experience of Learning and Teaching.* London: Karnac.

Sandler, J., & Sandler, A.-M. (1986) The gyroscopic function of unconscious Fantasy. In: D. Feinsilver (Ed.), *Towards a Comprehensive Model for Schizophrenic Disorders* (pp. 109–124). Hillside, NJ: Analytic Press.

Segal, H. (1957). Notes on symbol formation. *International Journal of Psycho-Analysis, 38:* 391–397.

Schacter, J. S., & Butts, H. F. (1968). Transference and Countertransference in interracial analysis. *American Psychoanalytic Association Journal, 16:* 792–808.

Sashidaran, S. P. (1986). Ideology and Politics in Transcultural Psychiatry. In: J. L. Cox (Ed.), *Transcultural Psychiatry* (pp. 158–178). London: Croom Helm.

Sherwood, R. (1980). *The Psychodynamics of Race: Vicious and Benign Spirals.* Brighton: Harvester Press.

Sinason, V. S. (1989). The Psycholinguistics of Discrimination. In: B. Richards (Ed.), *Crises of the Self, Further Essays on Psychoanalysis and Politics*. London: Free Association Books.

Steinbeck, J. (1939). *The Grapes of Wrath*. New York: The Viking Press.

Steiner, J. (1982). Perverse relationships between parts of the self: A clinical illustration. *International Journal of Psychoanalysis*, *63*: 241–251.

Steiner, J. (1993). *Psychic Retreats: Pathological Organisations in Psychotic, Neurotic and Borderline Patients*. London: Routledge.

Swaine, J. (12th August 2014). The Guardian: Michael Brown Shooting: "They killed another black man in America". Available at www.theguardian.com

Tan, R. (1994). Racism and similarity: paranoid-schizoid structures. *British Journal of Psychotherapy*, *10*: 31–43.

The New York Times (1993). Print Headline. "Rodney King Testifies About Night of Beating", 22nd January. Available at http://www.nytimes.com/1993/01/22/us/rodney-king-testifies-about-night-of-beating.html

Thomas, L. (1992). Racism and Psychotherapy; Working with Racism in the Consulting Room: An Analytical View. In: J. Kareem & R. Littlewood (Eds.), *Intercultural Therapy: Themes, Interpretations and Practice*. Oxford: Blackwell Scientific Publications.

Thomas, L. (1962). Pseudo-Transference Reactions Due to Cultural Stereotyping, *American Journal of Orthopsychiatry*, *32*: 894–900.

Timimi, S. (1996). Race and Colour in Internal and External Reality. *British Journal of Psychotherapy*, *13(2)*: 183–192.

Verrier, N. N. (1993). *The Primal Wound: Understanding the Adopted Child*. Maryland: Gateway Press.

Ward, I. (1988). New Introduction to White Racism. In: J. Kovel, *White Racism: A Psychohistory*. London: Free Association Books.

Ward, I. (1997). Race and Racism: A Reply to Sami Timimi. *British Journal of Psychotherapy*, *14(1)*: 91–97.

Winnicott, D. (1947). Hate in the Counter-transference. In: *Collected Papers: Through Paediatrics to Psychoanalysis*. London: Tavistock, 1958.

INDEX

For Product Safety Concerns and Information please contact our EU
representative GPSR@taylorandfrancis.com
Taylor & Francis Verlag GmbH, Kaufingerstraße 24, 80331 München, Germany

www.ingramcontent.com/pod-product-compliance
Lightning Source LLC
Chambersburg PA
CBHW052010270326
41929CB00015B/2859